GET TO KNOW
RON MARTIN

Here's what business people say about Ron Martin, his sales management system and his book,

Sales Management Made Easy ...

"Sales Management Made Easy delivers the message that it is a company's salespeople that insure its success. Ron Martin has demonstrated that belief to the employees of our 49 stores. This book is a must-read for all layers of management from the CEO to the entry level supervisor."

> – PAUL KOSASA
> *Vice-President*
> *ABC Stores*

"As usual, Ron Martin's style is straightforward and easy to read. The content is 'right on.' This is a great book. It addresses the issues that are most important to managers and gives them a strategy to remedy those concerns. The quotes add both humor and inspiration. The refrain, 'It's easy', punctuates each concept and reinforces that positive affirmation."

> – MARY K. FLOOD
> *Vice-President of Sales & Marketing*
> *Schuler Homes Inc.*

"If you want to build a world-class sales force, invest in Ron Martin's Success Made Easy series. His first three books may very well make the difference between your success and failure."

> – WYLAND
> *Environmental Artist*

"Ron Martin has certainly made success and selling *easy*. And now, he adds sales management to his trio of books. Each book is an *easy* read, and is filled with practical, specific tips to use immediately in both your life and business. I highly recommend this book to every sales manager and business owner.

Run, don't walk to your local bookseller!"

— JAN BERMAN
President
Retail Merchants of Hawaii

"An excellent new book from Ron Martin that every store owner should have."

— CLIFFORD D. SLATER
Chairman & CEO
Maui Divers of Hawaii, Ltd.

"Ron Martin's book, Retail Selling Made Easy, is the **'Retail Bible'** for our 11 stores. We give every employee a copy and all of our stores closely adhere to Ron's nine-step selling system and goal-tracking program.

With the publication of Sales Management Made Easy we now have a new **bible**. This book will be issued to every manager in our stores. I can finally sit back, put my feet up and let the money roll in!! Ron has done all the thinking and work."

— STEVE POGNI
Owner
Special Effects
Sausalito, Carmel, California

"Sales Management Made Easy offers a road map to success for any manager who is willing to read and follow the suggestions given throughout this book. While the book focuses primarily on retail sales management, I have been able to apply many of the principles directly to our wholesale operation."

— JEFF SWARTZ
General Manager
Booklines Hawaii

"Following two successful best sellers, Ron Martin's third book, Sales Management Made Easy, will most likely be a best seller too. This book is an essential guide that will help all sales managers motivate their salespeople to use a selling system that really works. Another great book by Ron Martin! I'm looking forward to the next one."

– WILLIAM A. WYLAND
President and CEO
Wyland Galleries Hawaii

"Ron Martin has done it again. Sales Management Made Easy is a practical tool for everyone who wants to be successful in business."

– VALERY O'BRIEN
Marketing Director
Horizon Group

"Truly outstanding! This is a book with incredibly direct applicable knowledge. It gives hope, direction and motivation to the struggling, as well as the successful, sales manager. And, it helps all of us in management to remain more focused on what we can do to improve the *top* line. Ron Martin's book is now required reading by all management personnel in our company."

– BRICK THOMPSON
CEO, Business Management Co., Inc.
Las Vegas, Nevada

"My company has grown along with Ron Martin through his work as a sales resultant, and reading his first two books. Sales Management Made Easy is his best work yet, and is a practical, hands-on tool for management growth."

– DAVE HAGERMAN
Hagerman Enterprises
San Francisco, California

"By following Ron's 'street savvy' our business has defied the small business high mortality rate — with ease."

– TERRY & ELIZABETH SNAVELY
Owners
Alohashells Hawaii

"With so many important tasks required to operate a business, it's easy to neglect the most important one — sales! Sales Management Made Easy shows you how to do it all — easily."

"I love Sales Management Made Easy. Ron Martin's books keep getting better. This newest book is now required reading at our company. Ron's systematic approach makes it *easy* to apply the Sales Management Made Easy principles, and get results."

"Salespeople perform better when they have a system to put the pressure on instead of themselves. Ron's system works for us!"

"Sales Management Made Easy redefines the word 'focus' as 'the key to sales success.' It has always meant that to me. Without a sales focus, the word 'management' would be meaningless."

"The ideas in Sales Management Made Easy apply not only to sales, but to everyone in supervision and management. I hope every supervisor in Maui County Government will read it".

County of Maui

"By working with Ron Martin, our sales manager has increased sales over 100% in the past year. Ron knows how to train sales managers. Now he has given you his system. You just need to follow his *easy* directions."

– JOHN PYLES
Owner
Mariners Alley Shopping Center
and
Golden Reef Jewelry Store
Lahaina, Maui

"Ron Martin unmasks the secrets of managing sales in Sales Management Made Easy. Sales Management Made Easy covers every detail and then prioritizes it. This book makes management *easy* while delivering increased sales."

– BERNARD VON NOTHAUS
Owner
Royal Hawaiian Mint

"Ron's concepts are contagious! After reading this book, in one sitting, I am saying, '**It's easy,**' at least 10 times a day!"

– PAM CHAMBERS
President
Pam Chambers Presentation Courses

"When we started using Ron Martin's sales and management techniques, we owned one Black Pearl Gallery. By incorporating Ron's systems and ideas, we have established six galleries in Hawaii and Nevada with our seventh opening soon in Miami, Florida!"

– DON KELLY
Owner and President
Black Pearl Gallery

"Sales Management Made Easy is a great addition to Ron's first two. This book will be a great benefit to everyone in business. I wish I had gotten all of this information when I started my retail art business over 35 years ago. But, I still benefit today by reading and rereading Ron Martin's books.

– BEVERLY FETTIG
Artist — Owner
Fettig Art Studios
Haleiwa, Hawaii

SALES MANAGEMENT MADE EASY

SALES MANAGEMENT MADE EASY

RON MARTIN

SUCCESS DYNAMICS

Library of Congress Catalog Card Number: 97-091659

First Printing 1997

10 9 8 7 6 5 4 3 2 1

Printed in the United States of America

In memory of my father Granville,
my wife Sarah, and my mother Frances.
All three left this earth a better place and while
here touched me as no others did or will.
Mahalo

Contents

Foreword

by Harold E. Johnson

Author • Mentoring For Exceptional Performance

Leadership is a subject we read a lot about in current management writings. Many authors are writing about it. Well, Ron Martin is actually living, modeling and mentoring a very pragmatic approach to a special kind of leadership — sales leadership. And, I have not seen anyone do the job any better than Ron.

My career has included being the CEO of six very different businesses. Ron and I worked together for about six years in one of these businesses. I observed that Ron had a world-class talent for making the all-important sales function hum. As he often said, and I would agree, "The financial cycle starts at the top line — revenue." And this is his specialty.

This third book of Ron's **Made Easy** series is not about general management. What is presented is a vividly concise look at **sales management**. Seldom does one find such a straightforward guide to successful sales management. For a world thirsting for success, Ron is holding a fire hose.

One of the aspects about Ron that I marvel at is how he breaks the sales function down into the critical parts. Then he teaches a system for successful selling that reproduces and multiplies his impact. And, now he does the same for sales management.

Fortunately, for those really interested in improving sales, Ron shares his success and selling secrets in his first two books. Now, the same is true for sales management. And he makes it look *easy* — which it is when you follow the leader.

Chapter 1

Managing Sales

Manage : "Handle, control ..."
— WEBSTER

As a Sales Manager, you must manage more than sales. You are expected to *handle* and *control* several important tasks, but none of your operational or administrative duties should ever take a higher priority than sales.

Handle Duties — Control Sales

Sales must be your number one priority. Managers who can *handle* duties are "a dime a dozen." Managers who can *control* sales are priceless.

When you control sales, you will always achieve your sales goals. You will succeed regardless of the obstacles and excuses that you encounter along the way. You control results.

 Control sales by influencing your salespeople to make selling their number one priority.

You influence your salespeople with your day-to-day behavior and communication. Your job is to *get* people to sell, not to *tell* them to sell.

Retail store managers are asked to handle an endless list of non-selling tasks which may include:

- Conducting inventories
- Stocking shelves
- Ordering stock
- Tagging merchandise
- Changing displays
- Meeting with vendors
- Calculating payroll
- Creating work schedules
- Conducting employee reviews
- Training salespeople
- Interviewing job applicants
- Preparing cost budgets
- Projecting sales
- Going to the bank
- Cleaning the store

You should never perform these duties at the expense of sales. A salesperson refolding T-shirts for the umpteenth time once said, "If my customers would just leave these T-shirts alone, I could keep them looking neat."

You buy, price, tag and display merchandise with one goal in mind, **to sell it!** You vacuum the carpet, clean the glass and polish the showcases in order to sell more merchandise.

Your goal is to attract, sell to, and keep your customers.

Control sales by making sales "the reason" for everything you do. Whenever you assign a task other than selling, tell your salespeople how the task will improve sales. For example, you could say:

● "Let's clean the windows today to make a better first impression and attract more customers."

● "Please tag this new merchandise as soon as possible so you can start selling it."

Success is pleasing your boss. Your salespeople want to please you, and nothing should please you more than sales.

Let's say you leave your store to go to the bank. You tell your salespeople: "While I'm gone, please inventory the under stock, clean the counter tops, vacuum the floor, tag these new items, and give every customer your undivided attention."

When you return from the bank you ask, "How's business?" Someone responds, "It's been slow." You look around and notice that the new items are tagged, the floor is vacuumed, the counter tops are clean, and the under stock has been inventoried. You are pleased. Your salespeople completed four of your five assignments. But, they missed the most important one — sales!

As a Sales Manager, you are responsible for creating the mind-set that *sales* matter most. Operational and administrative duties are *easy* to inspect. But, what about the unseen task? How do you know that business was "slow"? Did *every* customer receive your staff's undivided attention, or was everyone too focused on accomplishing the other four tasks?

 Inspect what you expect.

Expect sales, and inspect sales results. You will have more sales. **It's easy.**

To establish a followership, you must demonstrate leadership. Salespeople will rally behind a sales manager who knows where he or she is going. When your salespeople know that you are leading the way to success, they want to go with you.

When your salespeople know that your sales goal will be achieved, they want to be a part of it. They will do their share to assure your success.

Everyone wants to be a part of a winning team, and every winning team has a leader.

Chapter 2

Managing by Leading

*Lead: "To guide, to direct the operations,
activity or performance of ..."*

– WEBSTER

As a sales manager, your job is to *guide* and *direct*
the operations of your business as well as the activity and
performance of your salespeople. You are the leader.

The leader of the cavalry always rode the front horse.
When he pointed his sword forward and shouted,
"Charge!", his troops followed him. The leader never
looked back. His followers knew that he was heading for
victory. They wanted to be with him. There was no turning back.

What if this "leader" rode behind his troops, poked his
sword at them and hollered, "Charge!"? Everyone would
look back. No one would charge. They would see their
enemy in front of them instead of their charging *leader*.

*"If you run they will walk,
If you walk they will stop,
If you stop they will die."*

– FRENCH FOREIGN LEGION
OFFICERS MANUAL

To demonstrate leadership to his new officers, General George Patton would stretch a string across his desk and say, "Push the string over to me." As the young officer pushed the string towards General Patton, it collapsed, balled-up and went nowhere. Try it.

General Patton then picked up the string, and pulled it towards himself saying, "When you *pull* the string it *follows* in line." Try it.

The same is true when managing salespeople. Sales managers who push their salespeople do not sell as much as those who lead and pull. You "pull" when you lead by involvement and example.

 A struggling sales organization is often overmanaged and underled.

A retail store can achieve success and overcome any obstacle when there is leadership at the top. A store owner can solve money problems with a loan from the bank. If the location is poor, the store can be relocated. Poor salespeople can be replaced. Better merchandise can be purchased. But, if a store lacks leadership in its manager, it is doomed.

Leaders are visionaries. They see things as they can and will be, not merely as they are. Leaders convert their visions into reality. They achieve their sales goals. They inspire other people to join them.

"If you can dream it, you can have it."
– WALT DISNEY

• • •

"Some men see things as they are and say,
'why?'
I dream things that never were and say,
'Why not?'"
– ROBERT KENNEDY

• • •

Managers do things right – Leaders do the right things.

• • •

As a Sales Manager, you must do things right *and* do the right things. Your salespeople will follow the examples you set.

Leaders are both effective and efficient. Leaders gain the trust of their followers and use their influence to assure the success of their salespeople.

Most salespeople intend to do well. But, when things get difficult, their efforts and enthusiasm may wane.

The sales manager who is a leader keeps everyone focused on personal and store goals, guiding them over or around any obstacles they encounter.

● Leaders bring out the best in their salespeople by utilizing their strengths and overcoming their weaknesses.

● Leaders help their salespeople establish and reach personal and company goals.

● Leaders inspire their salespeople to continuously raise their personal goals, and then to exceed them.
● Leaders show the way to success.

Always lead by example. Have you ever heard the famous order: "Do as I say, not as I do"? Sorry, but that one doesn't work. Your salespeople will do as you do. People follow their leaders.

You set the example with **your** attitude, **your** appearance, **your** work habits, **your** selling approach and **your** sales results.

You can manage other people when you manage yourself. **It's easy.**

Chapter 3

Managing Yourself

"Self sacrifice enables us to sacrifice
other people without blushing."

– G. Bernard Shaw

You sacrifice certain rights when you become a manager. You lose your right to settle for mediocrity. You lose your right to complain or seek sympathy. You lose your right to sit back and wait for someone to tell you what to do. You lose your right to be a follower. You lose your right to fail.

Whether you realize it or not, your salespeople closely scrutinize your integrity and credibility. They notice how you *look*, how you *act*, and what you *say*.

Demand excellence from yourself, and you will get excellence from others. **It's easy!**

 Salespeople become mirror images of their sales managers.

When you follow your company's dress code and other policies, so do your salespeople. When you sell, so do your salespeople. **It's easy!**

The size of your store and sales staff may govern your personal selling opportunity. Some sales managers feel that they don't have the time to sell at all. Give yourself the luxury of selling, even occasionally. It will keep you sharp.

Some sales managers have adequate opportunity to sell, but don't. They don't like to, or don't want to, or are too busy handling duties.

To control sales, demonstrate sales potential. Occasionally tell your salespeople, "Today I am a salesperson. I wish I could sell all day everyday. Watch me."

 When you sell, you prove to your salespeople that selling is your top priority.

When you step onto the selling floor, you are leading by example. You gain respect. You give yourself the opportunity to say, "I'll show you how."

When *you* are selling no one can tell you: "It's slow" or "People aren't buying" or offer any other excuse. Your sales results prove that when you focus on sales, you sell.

Be sure to follow the same selling system that you teach to your salespeople. Demonstrate to your salespeople that your selling system works when it is followed. Excellence needs to be demonstrated.

 Manage yourself, then you can manage others.

Chapter 4

Managing Others

"The throne is but a piece of wood covered with velvet."

– NAPOLEON

Your management title does not automatically give you respect, or guarantee successful results. Sales managers who attempt to "stand behind" their titles often lose them.

Erika is a retail sales manager. She was overheard complaining: "None of my salespeople are reaching their goals. Should I fire them all?" In cases like this, it's usually the manager that gets fired.

 In professional sports, a losing team fires the manager, not the team.

New York Yankees' manager, Casey Stengel, managed professional baseball players for 25 years – 1935 to 1960. He managed more World Series wins than any manager in the history of baseball.

A sports writer once asked Casey Stengel, "How do you find so many great ball players?" Casey replied, "All major leaguers are great ball players. I just get them to play ball."

All of your salespeople can sell. It's your job to get them to sell. Telling them to sell is not sufficient. They must be taught, motivated, inspired, expected and led to sell.

Allowances and Expectancies

Your salespeople will get away with what they are allowed to, and do what they are expected to. You communicate your allowances and expectancies with what you say, as well as with what you don't say.

 What you don't say says as much as what you do say.

When someone fails to sell, and you fail to mention it, you *communicate:* "I understand. It's okay when you don't sell."

When one of your salespeople reports to work five minutes late, and you say nothing, you *communicate:* "That's okay." You wouldn't say, "That's okay" out loud, so don't say it silently. Your salespeople need to know the guidelines.

Developing good, successful, effective salespeople is much like raising good, honest, happy children. Children become mirror images of their parents' *allowances* and *expectancies*. In the process of growing, they test the limits.

Let's say you are the mother of a teenage son. He asks, "Can I go out with my friends tonight?" You answer, "Yes, but be home by midnight." He agrees.

Your son returns home at five minutes past midnight. He unlocks the front door wondering: "Is Mom up? What will she say? Am I in trouble?"

Let's say you're watching television. You're also watching the clock on the wall. You hear the door open. What you say and do next will *communicate* your true allowances and expectancies. Your rule has been broken. Your order has been ignored. Your son has disappointed you. You are angry.

You must communicate to your son that his behavior is wrong. But, you must do it with love. You must correct your son's behavior without damaging your relationship with him.

Many parents – and managers – overlook improper behavior in order to maintain good relationships. They develop good relationships with misbehaving or nonproductive children or employees.

Successful retailer Tom O'Gwynn tells every new employee: "I would like two things from you. Number one, do your job. And, number two, like me." Then he adds: "If I can't have both of my requests, give me the first one and I'll live without the second one."

Ideally your children and employees will do what you ask them to, *and* like you too. The second half of this equation is tested when your employee or child fails to do what you ask.

When your teenage son arrives home five minutes late, he knows he is wrong. But, it's *only* five minutes. It's no "big deal."

Let's say you realize he is only five minutes late, and lovingly say, "Hi honey, did you have a good time tonight?" He answers, "Yes, I did. Goodnight."

Your relationship is intact. But, you've created a problem. Your son has learned that "by midnight" can mean later than 12 o'clock. You've condoned his improper behavior. You've failed to help your son learn respect and compliance. You've allowed your son to change the rules and your expectancies. Your limits were not real after all.

Imagine a different scenario. When your son arrives home five minutes late, you growl, "You're late; 'by midnight' means before 12 o'clock! Go to bed, *and* you're grounded for a week!"

Have you altered your son's future behavior? Will your son think twice about being late again? Have you damaged your relationship with your son? The answer is yes to all three questions.

To alter improper behavior *and* maintain good relationships, you must be tactful and firm, yet caring. Demonstrate empathy, not sympathy.

 When you sympathize you paralyze.

Be empathetic. Seek a behavior change for the good of the other person. Communicate your message with warmth and understanding. You are truly sorry that you must address this situation, but you are going to.

The empathetic mother says to her slightly tardy son, "Hi, honey. Before you go to bed I need to talk with you. Please sit down."

Behavior modification begins immediately. He thinks: "I wish I had come home on time." Mom then asks, "What time do you have?" Her son replies, "Five after 12."

Mom asks, "What was our agreement tonight?" He meekly responds, "I said I'd be home by midnight." Mom kindly asks, "Why did you disappoint me?" He defends himself: "It wasn't my fault. I wasn't driving. I told my friends I had to be home by 12 o'clock sharp."

Mom continues, "Do you understand why it's important that you and I have a mutual trust? When we make a deal, you can count on me, and I can count on you. Okay?" Her son agrees. Mom then asks, "The next time you and I agree on something, can I count on you to honor our agreement?"

Anxious to conclude this brief, yet uncomfortable reprimand, her son says, "Yes." Mom adds, "Okay, goodnight. And one more thing, I love you. I'm sorry we had to have this little chat."

Can you recognize the key difference with this approach? Mom got her son to *admit* that his behavior was wrong. The key to mom's success was her careful use of *questions*, not demands and lectures.

 Reprimand with questions.

Some years ago, I met with a group of retail sales managers in California who were discussing how to control behavior, with empathy.

One of the sales managers, Betty, asked, "How do you control someone like Francis? He is our company's top salesperson. He is also a pain in the neck."

 Think of a difficult salesperson, who excels in sales, as a "pain in the *assets*."

Betty continued, "Francis won't follow the rules. He sets a bad example for everyone else. He stands outside the store and smokes. He knows that I don't allow that."

Someone asked, "Why *do* you allow it?" Betty responded, "I need his sales. He sells twice as much as anyone else does. But, I want him to follow my rules."

This sales manager is *allowing* Francis's unruly behavior because she needs his sales, but complaining about it behind his back rather than correcting it. Francis knows exactly what he can get away with. He is "managing his manager."

Betty explained what happened when her district manager caught Francis smoking and reprimanded him for it: "Francis quit, and I lost my number one salesperson."

Three weeks later Francis begged for his job back. He promised Betty that he would not smoke in front of the store again. You guessed it; he's number one in sales again, *and* he's smoking on the sidewalk again.

What if Betty were to emulate the empathetic mother with the tardy son? The next time Betty catches Francis smoking she says, "Francis, can I see you in my office please?" Francis extinguishes his cigarette and follows Betty into her office. Confidently, he is thinking, "I guess she hasn't looked at the sales results recently."

Betty says, "Have a seat, Francis." She asks, "What was the agreement we reached when you returned to work here?" Francis concedes, "I know, I said I wouldn't smoke in front of the store."

Betty asks, "Why did you disappoint me?" Francis responds, "I'm sorry, I forgot." Betty asks, "Do you understand why I do not allow smoking in front of the store?" Francis says, "Yes, it looks bad."

Betty continues, "Do you also understand why you and I must have a mutual trust? When I tell you you'll have a paycheck on Friday, you count on me, right?" Francis agrees. Betty then asks, "Can I count on you to follow this rule?" Francis reluctantly agrees.

As this five-minute meeting ends Betty says, "Okay Francis, one more thing. I really appreciate your sales. You're the best. I'm sorry we had to have this little chat. Have a great day."

Francis is likely to test Betty again and again. He *is* a "pain in the assets." Betty must always be willing to confront him with empathy and with questions.

If you follow this approach, and improper behavior continues, ask tougher questions, like, "Do you really want to work here?" or, "Do you fully understand my options to solve this problem?" or, "Can you understand that I'm growing tired of having these conversations?" or "What would you do if you were me?" or "Have you ever taken an IQ test?"

Your toughest salespeople will cave in and follow your rules provided you don't cave in and follow theirs.

Communicate your *allowances* and *expectancies* immediately and consistently. Tell your salespeople when you are pleased and displeased.

 Manage with a *verbal* mixture of "pats on the back, and boots in the rear ."

Catch your salespeople doing the right things. Reinforce proper behavior with a verbal "pat on the back." Say, "Way to go." Offer a visual "high five," or "thumbs up" when someone makes a big sale. Your salespeople develop discipline. They follow the systems that lead to their success.

Discipline is the essence of management. Discipline provides predictability. Predictability allows you to prepare for success.

When you develop discipline, your salespeople follow your company rules, policies and *selling systems.*

When you coach your salespeople to follow a proven system you are leading them to success.

When your salespeople follow your selling system, they sell more. Put pressure on your system to succeed, and on your salespeople to follow your system. **It's easy.**

"We are what we repeatedly do,
therefore excellence is not an act,
but a habit."

— ARISTOTLE

Chapter 5

Managing Priorities

Priority: "...Taking precedence logically or in importance."
— WEBSTER

"**W**ith so many things to do, and everything being important, where do I start?" When salespeople ask themselves this question, they sometimes do the wrong things first.

 Adopt a customer-based priority system that says: "Anything can wait, except our customers."

Make selling your number one priority. Put your customers at the head of the list. Your customers are more important to your business than duties. Without customers there would be no need for duties, salespeople or sales managers.

The organization chart at Nordstrom Department Stores shows the customer at the top and the company co-chairmen at the bottom. Nordstrom creates a culture that says: "Our business is servicing our customers." Nordstrom is famous for its outstanding customer service, and enjoys sales per square foot totals that are marveled by retailers everywhere.

When you telephone your store, always ask, "Are you with a customer?" When the answer is yes, say, "Good, I'll call you back," or "Good, call me when you are not with a customer."

Condition everyone in your office to always ask, "Are you with a customer?" And if so, to say, "Good, I'll call you back."

Remind your bookkeepers, secretaries, delivery staff, and anyone else working for you: "Everything we do is to service our customers."

When you enter your store, your first question should be, "How are sales?" If you get an adjective for an answer, ask for a number. When you hear, "Not too bad" or "Pretty good" or "Slow," ask, "How does that translate into dollars and cents?" Make numbers important and you'll achieve them. **It's easy.**

 Inspect sales first – then duties.

Make selling everyone's number one priority and you will have more sales – every day!

When you influence your salespeople to think: "Sell – Sell – Sell," you are controlling sales. Your salespeople are selling more to please you.

Make selling your primary goal, and your salespeople will be eager to perform any task you ask that leads to more sales.

Your salespeople will be more willing to clean your store windows to attract more customers. They will want to keep your store inventories current to allow more sales. They will enthusiastically vacuum, dust and polish your store to ensure good first impressions.

Salespeople who want to sell are anxious to study merchandise features and benefits, improve their selling skills, and attend training classes. They will do anything you ask that leads to more sales.

On the other hand, salespeople who are left alone to decide what to do first, may choose to do the easiest or most pleasant tasks first. Some salespeople become overwhelmed with all of the options and do little or nothing.

Talking to a customer should be the most pleasant task, but sometimes isn't. Some customers are cold and unfriendly. Salespeople experience rejection and disappointment when talking to many customers.

Let's say you just received a large delivery of T-shirts. You tell your salesperson, "Mary, when you are not with customers, please put these new T-shirts in the front window. Fold them neatly, and display them attractively so we can sell them today."

Mary looks around, doesn't see any customers in the store, and starts folding the T-shirts. Midway through her task, a customer enters the store. Mary greets her customer, and he coldly states, "I'm just looking!"

It's tempting for Mary to ignore this customer and finish folding the T-shirts. Her assumption is : "He doesn't want to talk to me. I have to finish folding these T-shirts. He will tell me if he wants something."

Proper behavior in this case is for Mary to back off, but remain *mentally* connected to her customer. The T-shirts are static, Mary's customer is dynamic. Her customer may be ready to talk to her at any moment. Mary must be ready for her customer when he is ready for her.

 The task will wait, your customer may not!

Establish and manage a customer-based priority system for your salespeople to follow. Several scenarios are possible.

Let's say you manage a retail store with one person selling at a time. Here is a simple 1 - 2 - 3 customer-based priority system:

Single Salesperson Priorities

- #1 - Servicing Customers
- #2 - Housekeeping
- #3 - Merchandising

Priority #1. Servicing Customers

Whenever there is a customer in your store, your attention should be on your customer. Greet your customers, give information, assist in their buying decisions and ring up sales. Ideally, in that order.

Priority #2. Housekeeping

When there are no customers in your store, do a quick housekeeping check. Look for displays that require straightening, out-of-place merchandise, or anything that has been dropped on the floor. Dust the counter tops and clean the glass. Do these tasks to get ready for your next customer.

When a customer enters your store, move to Priority #1.

Priority #3. Merchandising

When there are no customers in your store, and everything is in order, perform other assigned duties. Tag and stock your inventory. Create attractive merchandise displays. When a customer enters your store, move to Priority #1.

Your salesperson should be busy in the #1, #2, or #3 priority order at all times. When your salesperson is constantly in the #1 priority activity, you need more salespeople. **It's easy.**

As the manager of a one-person-at-a-time sales staff, it is your responsibility to keep each salesperson's priorities in order.

Take "mental snapshots" whenever you enter your store. Ask yourself, "Is my salesperson properly prioritized?" If so, your "mental snapshot" is in focus. If not, focus it by alerting your salesperson to the missed opportunity.

Your mere presence should influence your salesperson to do whatever is right. If not, demonstrate what to do. Make the sale yourself. You can talk with your salesperson later and point out why he or she should stay focused on the proper priority.

Multiple Salesperson A/B Priorities

If you are the manager of a store with several salespeople working together at the same time, consider this A/B Priority System. It works. **It's easy.**

Every salesperson is designated as either an A-Person, or a B-Person. Each has different priorities.

A-Person Priorities:

- **#1 - Cashiering**
- **#2 - Servicing Customers**
- **#3 - Housekeeping and Merchandising**

#1. Cashiering

Stay at the register when there are customers ready to checkout. Accurately record sales, suggest add-on items, thank customers for their purchases, and ask them to return.

#2. Servicing Customers

When customers are in your store, but not at the register, leave the register. Greet customers, give them information, and assist them in their buying decisions. While in the #2 priority activity, constantly watch the register area. Excuse yourself, and move back into your #1 priority activity as soon as a customer approaches the register.

#3. Housekeeping and Merchandising

When there are no customers in your store, perform assigned housekeeping and merchandising duties. When customers enter your store move into your #2 priority activity, then into #1.

B-Person Priorities:

- **#1 - Servicing Customers**
- **#2 - Housekeeping**
- **#3 - Merchandising**

#1. Servicing Customers

Whenever there are customers in your store, you should greet them, give them information, and assist them in their buying decisions.

#2. Housekeeping

When there are no customers in your store, inspect your store. Customers unfold merchandise, move store displays, drop trash and leave fingerprints on glass and showcases. Get your store ready for your next customer. When a customer enters your store, move into your #1 priority activity.

#3. Merchandising

When there are no customers in your store, *and* everything is in order, you should display, tag, fold or inventory merchandise as requested. When a customer enters your store, move to your #1 priority and greet your customer.

This A/B Priority System assures that every customer is someone's number one priority. When your A and B salespeople remain in their #1 priorities all day, you need more salespeople. **It's easy.**

A customer-based priority system gives your salespeople guidelines to follow. They know what to do. They don't waste time. This system allows you to *handle* duties and *control* sales.

A written customer-based priority system eliminates uncertainty. It prepares you to overcome unexpected obstacles.

Chapter 6

Managing Obstacles

*Obstacle: "Something that seriously
hampers action or progress..."*
—Webster

You success is either enhanced or hampered by your salespeople. Your salespeople are your biggest asset or your biggest liability. They hold the key to your success.

Achieving your sales goal every month is imperative, regardless of any obstacles you encounter. It would be wonderful if all you had to do was tell your salespeople, "Here's our goal. Surpass it." Your sales goal may be more important to you than to your salespeople.

 Many salespeople do not consider sales a career. It's often a means to an end – survival.

Your success as a sales manager may hinge upon the behavior and results of young, inexperienced and some-times, uncommitted salespeople.

Some people work in sales jobs because they don't know what else to do. Some are students working their way through school. Their schooling is probably more important to them than your sales. Others may be dropouts who couldn't, or didn't, finish school.

Some of your salespeople will have lofty goals, while some may have no goals at all. Some of your salespeople will have extensive sales experience, while others will have none at all.

Your salespeople will have different attitudes and ambitions too. Some will want *your* job some day, some may not want their own job today. Some of your salespeople expect to keep this job forever, while others may be looking for another one right now.

You can overcome these obstacles and achieve your sales goals by motivating everyone to succeed everyday. Make *your* goals and your *salespeople's* goals the same. Success breeds success. **It's easy.**

Engineering firms can hire trained engineers. They know what to expect. Accounting firms can hire experienced accountants. Ad agencies can recruit qualified account executives. Resumes can be closely scrutinized. References can be thoroughly checked.

Some great salespeople have no prior sales experience. For many people, sales is their first job. Inexperience in sales may be an obstacle; however, it is an even bigger blessing. Inexperience means no bad habits – yet.

Hire attitudes – offer experience.

Bruce Nordstrom, owner of Nordstrom Department Stores says, "We can hire nice people and teach them to sell. We can't hire salespeople and teach them to be nice."
– Robert Spector, *The Nordstrom Way* .

When you develop inexperienced, nice people into successful salespeople, your success is ***easy.***

 Expect the unexpected.

Examine your salespeople daily. Take their mental temperatures. Give them all a "checkup from the neck up." Their attitudes must be positive. Your salespeople are your life's blood.

Be prepared for excuses. When you hear: "It's slow," ask, "How can you speed it up?" This quick response reminds your salespeople that *they* control results. It focuses them back onto their behavior rather than excuses.

Some salespeople like to point the "finger of blame" at the weather, traffic, economy, competition or anything beyond their control.

 Salespeople who offer excuses are defeated by obstacles.

Sure the weather, traffic, economy and competition are factors, but so what? When the selling gets tough, the tough keep selling.

When someone points the "finger of blame," point your finger at something and say, "Look at my hand. When you point the 'finger of blame' at something there are three fingers pointing back at the solution – you!"

When your salesperson tells you, "It's slow," ask, "How many good customers do you need to have a good day?"

 All you need is one good customer to "make your day."

Your best customer of the *year* may enter your store just as your salesperson has decided: "People aren't buying." Because of this mind-set, your first-class customer fails to receive first-class customer service. You miss the sale. Your salesperson thinks, "I knew it – people aren't buying."

"I buy when salespeople sell."

– *Ted Turner*

 Your biggest obstacles to success are the fragile attitudes and work habits of your salespeople.

Mental attitudes can change throughout the day. Someone may start the day with a great attitude, and lose it by noon. Salespeople get their emotions battered around by their:

- Customers.
- Fellow salespeople.
- Managers.
- Competition.
- Personal lives.
- Fears.

This condition is normal. But, you must be aware of it and *control* it. Be prepared for "salesperson mood swings." When you detect depressed spirits, inflate them.

 There is nothing more depressing than a depressed person.

Never allow your customers to encounter a depressed salesperson. When you control moods and behavior you control results.

When you notice a lackluster attitude in one of your salespeople, ask, "Are you okay today?" If the answer is, "Yes," say, "Okay, I wasn't sure. Have a great day."

Your best salespeople will respond quickly to the slightest hint of your displeasure. They become "okay" immediately, and remain "okay" the rest of the day. They know that you are paying attention to them.

When your salesperson tells you, "I'm not okay," ask, "Is it personal, or is it business?" If the answer is "personal," ask, "Can you put it out of your mind and focus on your job, or do you need to leave to take care of it?" If your salesperson has a personal problem that is preventing sales, offer a choice, with empathy:

- Go home.

   Or

- Get focused.

The nature and details of someone's personal problem are none of your business. Everyone doing their jobs properly *is* your business.

When your salesperson tells you that the problem is business related, ask , "What is it?" It might be a dispute with a customer or another salesperson. It could be a conflict in scheduling. It might be something your salesperson can't do anything about. Find out what it is, then say, "Okay, I'll look into it. Now, can you get it out of your mind and focus on selling, or do you need some time off to keep thinking about it?" Offer a choice – with empathy:

- Go home.

   Or

- Get focused.

Other obstacles to your success can be unexpected resignations, salespeople who call in sick and "no shows."

 Your most costly salesperson is a missing salesperson.

You can expect some salesperson turnover. Good salespeople are in demand, and your best ones know it. When one of your salespeople suddenly quits and leaves you short-staffed, you lose sales. You cannot count lost sales. You cannot make up lost sales.

Make recruiting, training and motivating your sales management priorities, and you will overcome this and all other obstacles. Your salespeople will continue to improve. You will sell more.

 Sell to survive – recruit to grow.

You will always achieve your sales goals when you have the proper number of salespeople behaving in the proper manner, all of the time. **It's easy.**

You can adjust a salesperson's mood and motivation with a conversation, contest, challenge, reminder or threat.

The best way to prepare yourself for sudden resignations is to have other salespeople "in the wings." Live theater has standby actors and understudies behind the curtain, in the wings, learning the script. They are ready to step in if any actor falls ill, or fails to show up. The theater is prepared to succeed regardless of unforeseen obstacles. The show must go on.

Your "show" must go on too. You must achieve your sales goal with or without sufficient salespeople. It's easier with them. Expect the unexpected. Prepare yourself for success. Recruit better salespeople *before* you have to.

You always have an opening for someone better than your worst salesperson.

This "attitude" keeps you recruiting. This "attitude" keeps all of your salespeople striving to be better than the worst. When salespeople strive to be better, for any reason, they sell more.

Consider how successful you and your salespeople will be when, in spite of your constant search, your existing salespeople are better than any of the applicants.

The more you pay your salespeople, the more success you can demand of them. Professional athletes are paid very high salaries, and consequently great pressure is placed upon them to excel.

All professional sports teams have "the bench." They have more players sitting on the bench, hoping to play, than they have on the field actually playing.

All players in professional sports are replaceable, and they know it. They all know someone is preparing to take their jobs. They even know who it is. They all play harder and get better because of it.

 Never become satisfied, and you will never grow stale.

There are many sources for recruiting good salespeople. You can advertise in the Help Wanted section of your local newspaper. You can place tasteful signs *inside* your store. You can share job opportunities in your company with people you meet.

An excellent way to recruit is by offering your existing salespeople a bonus or reward for referring someone to you. Your existing salespeople know the job. They may know someone who is perfect for the job.

When you are always recruiting, and everyone knows it, magic happens. Your existing salespeople stay on their toes. And, you have a constant stream of qualified applicants to consider should someone quit. **It's easy.**

Chapter 7

Managing With Incentives

"Geese that lay golden eggs don't work for chicken feed."
– RON MARTIN

Selling is the most incentive-laden profession there is. Salespeople are paid salaries, commissions, bonuses and overrides. Good salespeople can earn as much money as doctors and lawyers do. They don't need a formal education, or have to work 60 hours a week.

Some people go to college and earn degrees in engineering, accounting, law or business, then take a selling job. Why? Because they can make more money in less time.

Many retailers and service companies pay their salespeople more money than most companies pay their professional employees. They do so for good reasons. Salespeople need incentives.

Incentive: "Something that incites or is likely to incite determination or action."
– WEBSTER

Incentives incite your salespeople into action.
Incentives keep them determined to succeed.

In many professions a good salary is sufficient incentive
to show up at work and do a good job. Salespeople must
do more than show up and do a good job. To excel, salespeople must want to succeed – every day. They have to
start at $0 every day.

 **Incentives encourage
exceptional behavior.**

Selling is occasionally difficult or unpleasant. You must
talk with people you wouldn't socialize with. You must be
friendly to people who are not always friendly in return.
You face constant rejection and disappointment.

Without sufficient incentive to face your next customer,
you may turn your attention to the other duties you must
perform. You may become reactive to your customers
rather than pro-active.

Most salespeople do not have sales managers watching
over their shoulders, scrutinizing their every word and
move. Even with a customer-based priority system in place,
your salespeople get to decide whether to talk to a customer
or fold a T-shirt. Most of the time, no one is watching.

 **Without incentives or watch-dog bosses,
salespeople become inactive and reactive
in order to avoid rejection.**

Incentives make the potential rejection worthwhile. Incentives make your customers most important. Incentives remind salespeople of their first priority – selling.

Salesperson incentives are one reason that Nordstrom's customers are so loyal. Nordstrom salespeople belie the belief that commissioned salespeople are pushy salespeople.

Brick Thompson is a successful CEO in Las Vegas. Brick sums it up. He says, "I'll sure be glad when Nordstrom has a store in Las Vegas. I go all the way to Los Angeles when I want to shop." That's customer loyalty.

Establish an incentive program based on sales results and you'll get the results you want. Your salespeople will want the same results that you do. You are a team. **It's easy.**

Your incentive program is your "velvet-covered hammer" to motivate your salespeople to excel. Your incentive program is a positive prod that stimulates proper behavior, and consequently higher sales.

Your incentive program allows you to broadcast on the same frequency that your salespeople listen to. A common analogy is that everyone is tuned to the same FM radio station. It is WIIFM—**What's In It For Me?**

Your management requests are filtered through WIIFM. Your salespeople think: "What's in it for me?"

When your salesperson hesitates to stop performing an important task in order to talk to a customer who may not buy, your success is at stake. When your salesperson thinks: "Should I or shouldn't I?", WIIFM is playing loudly.

Your incentive program allows you to "broadcast" on WIIFM. When you ask your salespeople to adhere to your customer-based priority system, you can add, "And you will make more money."

There are many ways to structure incentive programs. Incentive programs can be on-going or short-term. Both work.

Incentive programs can be based upon personal performance, team performance or both. Incentive programs can be based upon daily, weekly, bi-monthly or monthly results. They all work.

Incentive programs can be based upon total sales, average sales, increased sales, new sales, sales per hour, sales per day, sales per week, sales per month or sales per year. Pick one – they all work!

Incentive rewards to your salespeople can be in the form of a percentage of their sales or a salary increase. Rewards can be paid daily, weekly or monthly.

Your incentive program will be unique to your store or business. The type of merchandise you sell, your location and your profit margins are all factors in determining how much to invest in salesperson incentives.

 The degree of salesmanship needed to "ring the cash register" is your most important consideration.

The incentive program for a fast food restaurant should be much different from that of a jewelry store. Here are some options to consider when creating your unique incentive program.

Salary Only Incentive Program

A salary only incentive program can work, but remember WIIFM. When your salespeople ask themselves, "What's in it for me?", the answer is, "I get to keep my job." To some the answer may be: "I will get recognition, a raise or promotion some day." But, to most it's, "I can keep my job."

 When keeping your job is your main motivator, it had better be a *great* job, especially when it's a selling job.

A salary only incentive program works best in a sales environment with several salespeople working together. A busy sales floor usually has a full-time sales manager to supervise priorities and behavior.

 A high salary allows you to hire good people. A good manager keeps good people doing a good job.

Salary/Plus % **Incentive Program**

There are many benefits in salary/plus % incentive programs. You can offer someone a better opportunity with a lower salary than you can with a salary only program.

While guaranteeing a lower salary, you are also offering a higher total earnings potential. But, only with increased sales. Win/win. **It's easy.**

Let's say you are budgeted to pay a salesperson $8 per hour to sell T-shirts. That's $320 in payroll for 40 hours, regardless of sales.

With a salary/plus % incentive program you might offer $6 per hour plus 2% of personal sales. You are now guaranteeing a $240 salary instead of $320. Your salesperson's earnings however, are not limited to his or her salary.

For a salesperson to earn $320, he or she must sell a total of $4,000 in T-shirts for the week:

Example: salary: $6 x 40 hrs.   = $240

Plus

commission: 2% x $4000   = $ 80

Total Earnings   = $320

If T-shirt sales for the week are only $3,000, your salesperson still earns more than your $6 per hour guarantee, yet your labor cost is less than the $8 per hour you are budgeted to pay. Win/win.

Example: salary: $6 x 40 hrs.   = $240

Plus

commission: 2% x $3000   = $ 60

Total Earnings   = $300

But, when this incentive program *incites* your salesperson to talk to more customers, follow your selling system, try harder, be nicer, and care more – everyone wins. Everyone makes more money. **It's easy.**

Example: salary: $6 x 40 hrs.   = $240

Plus

commission: 2% x $8,000   = $160

Total Earnings   = $400

In this case, your salesperson earned $160 more than your guaranteed $6 per hour. The biggest difference is $4,000 more in your cash register. Win/win.

In the above example, your $6 per hour salesperson is actually earning $10 per hour, and you're happy to pay it.

"Plus 2%" may not be the right formula for your store or business. Do the arithmetic and find out. Maybe it's 2%, maybe it's 1% or 10%. You're unique. The question is, "What percentage of *extra business* are you willing to offer to get it?"

Another variable you can add to a *salary/plus* % incentive program is a sliding scale. Here's how it works.

Example: **Salary/Plus**

   $0-$8,000   + 2%   = Maximum Bonus: $160
   $8-$10,000   + 2.5% = Maximum Bonus: $210
   $10-$12,000   + 3%   = Maximum Bonus: $270
   $12-$15,000   + 4%   = Maximum Bonus: $390
   $15,000 and up   + 5%   = Maximum Bonus: no limit

Would you rather pay a salesperson $320 for $4,000 in T-shirt sales, or $630 for $15,000 in T-shirt sales? Do the arithmetic.

Salary/*or* % Incentive Program

A salary/*or* % program offers a low salary *or* a high percentage of sales, whichever is greater.

Ideal candidates for this type of incentive program are high-end, high margin retailers such as jewelry stores, furniture stores, art galleries and specialty boutiques. These businesses must control labor costs, but also require the best salespeople.

 A salary/*or* % incentive program feeds the winners and starves the losers.

"Salary/ *or* %" incentive programs protect your company's downside while offering a high upside to your salespeople. The only necessity for everyone to win is *sales*. "Salary/ *or* %" means: win/win *or* lose/lose.

Confident, self-motivated salespeople thrive on this form of incentive. When offered the choice of a salary, or a high %, they take the high % every time.

"Salary/*or* %" incentive programs screen out many of the losers with the low salary guarantee. They cannot recognize the true potential or they know they are not capable of achieving it.

Example: **salary - $5.50 per hour *or* 10% of sales**

$5.50 x 40 hours	= $220
	OR
sales at 10% x $1,000	= $100
Total Earnings	= $220

In the above example, your $5.50 per hour guarantee represents a selling cost of 22%. Had this same salesperson been guaranteed $8 per hour, your selling cost would be 32%. Your goal in this example is to keep your selling cost at 10%. When you do, everyone makes more money. Win/win.

The salesperson in the above example *earned* only $100 (10%) but was paid $220 (22%). This earned/paid ratio should always be discussed with every salesperson on pay-day. All of your salespeople must "pay their way."

On the positive side, your salespeople can earn much more than $5.50 per hour. When they do, your labor per-cent becomes controllable – 10%. The more you pay your salespeople the happier you are.

Example: **salary - $5.50 per hour x 40**   **= $220**

                                           OR

           sales at 10% x $3,000   = $300

           Total Earnings   = $300

In this case, 10% of sales amounts to $7.50 per hour for your salesperson. There is no cap on your salesperson's earnings, and your labor cost is controlled – 10%.

Example: **salary - $5.50 per hour x 40**   **= $220**

                                             OR

           sales at 10% x $10,000   = $1,000

           Total Earnings   = $1,000

This salesperson *earned*, and was paid $25 per hour. Your labor cost is still only 10%. Win/win.

If you are budgeted to spend 10% on selling labor, and all of your salespeople are earning more than their guaranteed hourly rate, everyone wins. **It's easy.**

 You can have as many salespeople as you want as long as they all "pay their way."

Flushing out the losers is crucial to the success of a salary/*or* % incentive program. Those who cannot earn the budgeted % cannot stay!

Have a face-to-face "paycheck meeting" with every salesperson on every pay day. Say, "Did you pay your way?"

People who don't pay their way increase your labor costs. Their high cost of labor makes it difficult for you to reward your winners. You can't let the weeds choke out the flowers.

% Only Incentive Program

The minimum wage law in the United States prohibits paying "% only" to *employees* unless the total amount paid is more than the current minimum wage.

 Retailers who pay % only may be breaking the law.

You must guarantee minimum wage and other legal benefits to all of your employees, unless they are independent contractors. Independent contractors are not employees.

Independent contractors cannot be told what to do, or how and where to do it. You cannot legally provide independent contractors with an office, a store, a car or a telephone, unless they pay for it.

The systems offered in this book are intended to motivate and develop salesperson *employees,* individually and as a team.

Team Incentive Programs

When considering using a team incentive program ask yourself: "How many salespeople are required, at one time, to make a sale?"

Some salespeople have the luxury, or responsibility, of handling their customers from start to finish, all by themselves. If this is the case, a personal incentive program is all that you need.

In some cases, customers require the involvement of more than one salesperson. Some selling floors have several customers and salespeople interacting with one another.

Your selling system might dictate that your salespeople remain in assigned sections of your store while customers roam freely. Your customers encounter more than one salesperson. Individual sales cannot be tracked fairly. Team incentives work best in situations like this.

Stores using the A/B customer-based priority system offered in Chapter 5 are prime candidates for a team incentive program.

To establish a team incentive program ask yourself:

- "How much do I *need* to sell this month?"
- "How much do I believe I *can* sell this month?"
- "How much do I believe I *will* sell this month?"

Let's say your answers are: I need to sell $80,000 – I believe I can sell $100,000 – I believe I will sell $80,000. In this example, your team incentive program must increase your sales beyond $80,000 for the month.

You tell your sales team: "History says that if we continue to do what we have been doing, our sales will be $80,000 this month. I believe we can sell $100,000, and I am willing to pay you to help me prove it." Here's how:

Over The Goal Team Incentive Program
Goal $80,000

Incentive: 5% of all sales over the goal. The reward will be divided based on the % of total hours each person works during the month.

Immediately, everyone on your team wants to work more hours and create more sales. Most important, everyone wants to exceed your $80,000 goal.

Let's say your team consists of five salespeople and together they sell $90,000 for the month. That's $10,000 over your goal.

$$5\% \times \$10,000 = \$500$$

Your team divides $500. If everyone works an equal number of hours, everyone gets $100. You get $10,000 in added sales. Win/win.

A team member who is part-time and only works 10% of the total hours gets 10% of the bonus – $50. In this case your four full-time salespeople get $112.50 each. **It's easy.**

The incentive is an extra payday for your salespeople. They know that when they achieve $100,000 in sales, which you ultimately want, their bonus will be $1,000. When this is achieved, you receive $20,000 in added sales. Your added cost is $1,000. Do the arithmetic.

% *Team* Incentive Program

This approach *guarantees* everyone a bonus without achieving any particular goal.

Example:	%	sales	Maximum Bonus
	.05 %	$ 0- 50,000	– $250
	1 %	$50- 75,000	– $500
	2 %	$75,000-100,000	– $1,000
	3 %	over $100,000	– unlimited

The % team incentive program guarantees your salespeople a bonus even if you miss your goal, but even more when it is achieved and exceeded. When your team sells $100,000 your added cost is $1,000. But, as your team sells more than $100,000 in a month, your bonus cost is fixed at 3% on the extra sales.

Personal and team incentive programs can be based on hourly, daily, weekly, and/or yearly results. All work, but realize:

The tighter the measure the higher the productivity.

When you manage the minutes, you control the hours. Make every day count, and you can count on achieving your monthly goal.

Good incentives can sometimes become routine and commonplace. Keep your incentive program fresh in every salesperson's mind, and spice things up with timely contests.

Chapter 8

Managing Contests

"I can resist everything except temptation."

— OSCAR WILDE

Contests *tempt* your salespeople to set higher goals, try harder and sell more. Contests inspire your salespeople to compete. Spirited, well-managed competition is healthy. Contests are fun, and they keep everyone focused on achievement.

Anytime you want to boost sales, have a contest. Contests give your top performers the recognition they expect and deserve. Contests prove possibilities.

"We manage by contest."

— BRUCE NORDSTROM

 Salespeople will try harder for recognition than they will for money alone.

Contest results demonstrate potential. Contests institutionalize example-setting.

Contests can be based upon short-term or long-term results. Contests can reward winners with lavish prizes or inexpensive ego-boosting recognition. Contests can provide prizes for your top performers or for everyone.

You can spend a lot of money on contests, or very little. All contests should increase your sales above the norm, and make money for you and your salespeople. **It's easy.**

As you create sales contests, be sure to differentiate between your normal selling incentives and your periodic contests. Your ongoing commission and bonus programs are "for sure" incentives. Contests enhance everyone's everyday opportunity.

 Contests can stimulate sales of an exciting new product or move out old or overstocked merchandise.

Contests can be structured to beat last year's total sales, sales per month or sales per hour. Contests can create competition between your salespeople, and/or teamwork among them. Contests work.

The presentation of your sales contest to your salespeople is more important than the actual structure of your contest. Your presentation of the prizes is more important than their monetary value.

Always explain your contest to your salespeople in a group meeting or team rally. Add "hoopla" to your announcement, and you will create added interest and make it fun.

Sell your team on your contest. Group excitement and acceptance motivate lesser achievers to participate.

Kick off your contest with a team rally, and inspire competition.

Always present prizes to winners at your team rally for everyone to see. Reward past winners, as you announce future contests. It's exciting, motivational and fun.

When you present prizes in public, the recognition becomes more valuable than the actual prize. Small trophies or framed certificates have enormous value when presented ceremonially.

Your two primary considerations for a contest are:

- Desired Results
- Contest Budget

 Properly structured sales contests pay for themselves with increased sales. Good contests make you money.

Some sales managers say, "We don't have a budget for contests." Such thinking is like looking through the wrong end of a telescope. What if someone offered you $100, and asked for just $10 in return. Would you say, "I don't have $10 in my budget."?

Budgets can be restrictive. It's easy to think about the costs of a contest. It's just as easy to turn the telescope around and focus on the potential boost in sales.

Never assume that you would have had the same sales without your contest. If your sales are not higher, your contest was poorly designed, implemented or promoted.

 Make all of your contests:
"Do it and get it" or "Do it and hope to get it."

Do it and Get it

"Do it and get it" contests are objective. They reward your top performers. Salesperson of the Month and Store of the Month contests often reward the same salesperson or store manager repeatedly. As a result, some people lose their motivation to compete. Everyone knows in advance who is going to win.

You can have ongoing Salesperson of the Month awards that are not costly. This approach gives you a budget to create other contests that motivate everyone else.

 Top performers are proud to collect
#1 trophies, plaques and pins when they are
presented with thunderous applause from
their peers.

Another "do it and get it" contest is setting a specific sales goal for every salesperson, and offering a specific prize for achieving the goal. The goal and prize can be different for each salesperson, or they can be the same.

You might say, "All salespeople who sell more than $10,000 this month will receive an extra 5% on all sales over $10,000. Go for it." Keep it dynamic. Say, "Do it and get it."

You can offer prizes for selling certain products. You can say, "Sell one of these and you win..." or "Sell 100 of these this month and you win..."

"Do it and get it" contests have unpredictable costs. When you say, "Everyone who sells 10 of these wins," you don't know how many people will win.

Structure your "do it and get it" contests with more winners and smaller prizes than your "do it and hope to get it" contests.

Do it and hope to get it.

"Do it and hope to get it" contests can offer much larger and more exciting prizes to fewer winners.

You control the number of winners. You may have only one winner, but you can still keep everyone competing and selling more all month, right up to the last hour of the last day.

You might say, "Every time you sell one of these you get a chance to win a trip to Las Vegas" or "Every day that your sales exceed this goal you get a chance to win this new television set" or "Every transaction you have over $100 gets you another ticket in the drawing for $1,000 in cash."

"Do it and hope to get it" contests keep everyone involved until the very end. Your cost is predictable because you decide the prize in advance. You are happy to see anyone win. **It's easy.**

"Do it and hope to get it" contests sometimes disappoint top salespeople. Their tickets are not drawn even though they accumulate the most tickets. They forget that they also make the most money.

Managing disappointed contenders is part of your job. Remind your disappointed top salesperson: "*You* win every day and every month, contest or no contest. If everyone sold like you, I wouldn't need a contest."

The best contests combine "do it and get it" elements with those of "do it and hope to get it." They are easy to explain and understand. For example:

This Month's Contest

Salesperson of the Month	#1 Trophy + $50
2nd & 3rd Place	$20 bonus each

On Time Drawing

Achieving personal monthly goal	= 10 tickets
Working all assigned shifts	= 5 tickets
Daily sales over $1000	= 2 tickets
Every sale over $100	= 1 ticket

3 Winners will be drawn at our next Rally
Must be on time to win.

1st Name Drawn – $100 Bonus
2nd Name Drawn – $50 Bonus
3rd Name Drawn – $25 Bonus

Your costs are fixed. You can add importance to anything you want accomplished by offering additional tickets in the drawing. **It's easy.**

Promote Your Contest

Your sustained excitement for the duration of your contest is essential. This contest was created to motivate *everyone* to:

● Strive to be #1, #2 or #3.
● Achieve personal goals.
● Work all assigned schedules.
● Target on $1,000 days.
● Target on $100 transactions.
● Arrive on time for the next rally with lots of tickets in the drawing.

Benefits of this Contest

Your company wins because:
● Everyone focuses on sales.
● You have added morale.
● You boost your sales.

Your salespeople win because they:
● Focus on sales.
● Receive recognition.
● Have fun.
● Sell more.
● Make more money.

Some of your salespeople will give up on one or more of their goals as the month progresses. You must focus their attention on some other target that is still attainable. Keep your contest alive. Tell everyone how everyone else is doing. Tell *everybody* the score, everyday.

Keeping score makes it fun. It makes it a game. How long would you play tennis, golf, volleyball or any other game without keeping score?

Provide continuous contest feedback.It can be one-on-one or through a company publication. Tell everyone, everyday who's in first, second and third place. Tell everyone who is exceeding their personal goals.

Recognize those who have not missed a selling shift. Highlight those salespeople who have had $1,000 days and $100 transactions. Tell *everybody* the score, everyday.

Tell everybody how many tickets each person has in the drawing so far, how many days are left in the month to get more, and add, "Good luck."

 Salespeople get lucky when they try harder.

Chapter 9

Managing Training

Train: "To form by instruction, discipline or drill ..."
— WEBSTER

As you instruct, discipline and drill your salespeople, keep in mind that knowledge is power. As you teach your salespeople how to look, how to act, and what to say, you give them power.

Salespeople must feel confident and powerful when they approach their customers. They have power when they know what to expect, how to act, what to say and what to do to produce more sales.

 Selling is a *skill*. It must be taught, practiced and monitored.

Sales training never ends. Good habits must be reinforced. New techniques and better ways of selling demand constant learning and teaching.

By the time athletes become professionals, they have been well *trained*. They know how to play the game, but their coaching continues throughout their careers.

The higher you rise in the ranks of professional sports, the more coaching you get.

Professional baseball teams employ a general manager, field manager, first base coach, third base coach, pitching coach, batting coach and more. All of these coaches teach and motivate professional athletes who have multi-million dollar salaries to strive for excellence.

Some sales managers assume that a couple of hours or days of training is sufficient. It's not! Some sales managers assume that training is not important. It is!

Some companies use the "religious approach" to sales training. They hire salespeople and pray to God they sell something.

Some things should be taught before your new salespeople face their first customers. You should establish a formal orientation process that teaches every new salesperson how to sell.

Orientation Training

Print a checklist that covers everything your salesperson needs to know to make a sale. Go through this list with every new salesperson. **It's easy.**

Document your selling procedures.

Selling procedures are automatic to you, but they may be awkward at first for your new salespeople. Make it easy for your new salespeople to study, observe and practice sales techniques before meeting their first customers.

Your orientation training should include role-playing sessions with mock selling situations. Find out what your salespeople are prepared to say before they say it to your customers.

Your orientation training should teach your selling system first. Practice sessions, open book quizzes, selling observations and role-playing all imprint your selling system into your new salesperson's mind.

Once your salespeople have passed this "dress rehearsal" they can sell to real customers and enter into the ongoing phase of their training – coaching and motivating.

Formal training classes and informal coaching sessions are the cornerstones of your ongoing training program.

Formal Training Classes

Formal training should be conducted classroom style, away from customers and potential interruptions. Hold regularly scheduled training classes for both your new *and* experienced salespeople. These training classes can be scheduled weekly or monthly.

Experienced salespeople should be required to attend class whenever their sales fall below a certain level. Everyone should be required to attend class when you have a new product, promotion or contest.

Regularly scheduled training classes institutionalize ongoing learning and growth.

Plan your training agenda in advance and follow it. Keep your training fresh, positive and motivational. Regularly scheduled training classes offer you the opportunity to:

- Teach your selling system.
- Motivate your salespeople to follow your selling system.
- Offer contest updates.
- Share success stories.
- Role-play.
- Give quizzes.
- Sell your opportunity.

Keep your formal training classes short. An hour is a long time to sit and listen to anyone, or to be away from selling.

Prepare a three-hour agenda, then present it in one hour. Make it fun. Your salespeople will look forward to your training classes.

Informal Coaching Sessions

Clara is an outstanding salesperson. She sells fine art. Her manager, Tamara, was observing her when a customer entered the art gallery. He paused to look at a framed painting on an easel.

Clara rushed up to her customer and said, "That frame is made of koa wood, which grows in Hawaii. We have the highest quality, best selection, and the lowest prices." When Clara paused and took a breath, her customer said, "Yes, it's nice, but I need to think about it. I'll be back," and he left the gallery.

Tamara asked Clara, "How many steps in our selling system did you skip with that customer?" Clara thought and answered, "Four." Smiling, Tamara said, "Right!"

Questions control thought. Control your salespeople with questions. Coach with questions. This outstanding salesperson knew what to do, she just didn't do it this time. She skipped four important steps in her system. She didn't greet her customer properly, position herself appropriately, sell herself and relax her customer. She went right for the sale.

It wasn't long before another customer entered the art gallery. Clara looked her customer in the eye, smiled and said, "Aloha." She quietly observed her customer's reaction. Her customer started asking questions, and within minutes, Clara was ringing up a big sale.

This great salesperson was back on track, doing a great job, and making more money. It took less than a minute of empathetic coaching from Tamara to give Clara a long-lasting habit adjustment, and a raise in pay.

 Informal coaching sessions should be specific, fast, positive and effective.

Demonstrate – Coach – Critique

Here's your chance to sell, train, motivate and build credibility for yourself all at the same time. While coaching, tell your salesperson, "Okay, the next customer is mine. Watch, listen and make notes of what I do right or wrong. Be prepared to tell me how I made or lost the sale."

Some sales managers avoid demonstrating how to sell because they fear they might not make a sale. So what? Everyone misses sales. Prove to your salespeople that you are not perfect or afraid of rejection. Prove to your salespeople that your system can be followed regardless of whether the sale is made or not.

 Selling is *giving* your customer sufficient information to make an intelligent buying decision – yes or no! It's easy.

When your customer departs, critique your performance with your new salesperson. Discuss how you made or missed the sale.

After demonstrating, coach. Say, "Okay, the next customer is yours. Remember, first impressions and timing are important. Go!"

As your salesperson sells, watch and listen. Think and make notes. When the customer departs, critique your salesperson's performance. Show your salesperson where the sale was made, or missed.

Demonstrate – Coach – Critique. **It's easy.**

"*Those having torches will pass them on to others.*"

– PLATO

Chapter 10

Managing Communication

Communicate: "...To make known."

– WEBSTER

Executives are paid good money to come up with good ideas. Sometimes they fail to communicate their good ideas to their good people who can turn them into good results.

Have you ever played the communication game where someone reads a story, then whispers it to someone else? The story is whispered around the room and finally repeated out loud by the last person to hear it.

Sometimes the story changes so dramatically that it is unrecognizable. Facts become distorted and exaggerated. Individual interpretations become facts.

This same phenomenon occurs when high-paid sales executives "hatch" a new idea and then pass it on to their front-line salespeople. Communication sometimes breaks down somewhere between the top and the bottom.

Salespeople have the biggest impact on sales. Sales managers have the biggest impact on salespeople.

Communicate your goals, allowances and expectancies directly to your salespeople. Expect them to understand you, then inspect what you expect. **It's easy.**

You have a lot of information to communicate to your salespeople in addition to your sales goals. There is always something new to sell, and new information to be learned. Sales campaigns, promotions, specials, contests, assignments and messages must all be communicated to your salespeople.

I conduct monthly "Success Rallies" for shopping centers. The rallies are provided by the shopping centers, and offered free of charge to all merchants and their salespeople.

Salespeople who regularly attend these rallies develop a positive attitude and learn a selling system that works. They make more money.

Invariably, those salespeople who are "missing success" are also missing at these "Success Rallies." When asked why, they often say, "I didn't hear about it," or "Nobody told me."

 It's your responsibility to communicate everything that's important to all of your salespeople.

Some communications systems that you can use are:
- A communication book.
- A Key Person Communication form.
- A company newsletter.
- Memos.
- Meetings.
- Personal visits.
- Audio or video tapes.
- The telephone.
- The fax machine.
- E-mail.

Use any or all of these systems to establish an effective flow of communication in your business. Remember: *Every system requires a master.* You are the master of your systems. Inspect what you expect.

Communications Book

A composition book or three-ring binder makes an ideal communication system.

Label the book "Communication" and keep it handy in your store or sales office. Require all of your salespeople to review and initial the communication book at the beginning of every selling shift.

Your communication book should include:
- Sales updates.
- Contest standings and results.
- Recognition for high sales.
- Assignments.
- Messages.

Update your communication book daily. Use colors and graphics to make it fun and interesting. Apply stick-on "happy face" messages to recognize a big sale or a big day.

Once your salespeople get hooked on reading your communication book, you've mastered communication. **It's easy.**

Key Person Communication

Identify your most important employee, then establish a written flow of communication with that person alone. The Key Person Communication form benefits you and your key person. Communication is in place even if you travel. Nothing is overlooked. Key people are busy. By using the Key Person Communication form your key person doesn't have to remember to tell you something important. And, you are compelled to respond when you are informed.

Key people are vital to your success, and you are vital to theirs.

The Key Person Communication form is simply handed or faxed daily between key people.

It works. **It's easy.**

Company Newsletter

Company newsletters are valuable, especially to companies that have multiple locations. Newsletters can be published and distributed weekly, monthly, quarterly and or yearly. They all work.

KEY PERSON COMMUNICATION

TO:

FROM: DATE:

TIME	LOCATION	OBSERVATIONS	ACTION NEEDED	RESPONSE
8AM				
9AM				
10AM				
11AM				
NOON				
1AM				
2AM				
3AM				
4AM				
5AM				
6AM				
7AM				
8AM				
AFTER 8PM				

ADDITIONAL COMMENTS: _____
_____
_____
_____
_____

Make your newsletter fun and interesting to read. Use lots of photographs. When salespeople receive a company newsletter they immediately look for their own pictures. Next, they look for their names, then something about their store. Finally, they read other important stories.

Your newsletter should contain tips on selling, information about new merchandise, contest results, company announcements, articles by company officers, and human interest stories about company employees.

A company newsletter gives you the opportunity to put your employees' names and faces in print. It's recognition at the highest level. It's inexpensive, it motivates people. And, **it's easy.**

Memos

 The written word often escapes the racing mind of the salesperson.

Salespeople earn their money by talking. Some great salespeople make terrible accountants or business people. Some don't even balance their checkbooks.

Many salespeople don't read for pleasure, and resist reading for business. Keep the above thoughts in mind as you write memos to your salespeople.

Keep memos to salespeople short and easy to read. Include a section to: "Initial and fax back" or "Read and initial."

Meetings

Salespeople hate going to meetings. Why? Because there are no customers there. Good salespeople want to sell. Some salespeople consider any other activity a waste of their time and opportunity.

In spite of this resistance, meetings are valuable. Meetings give you the opportunity to see your team assembled as one.

Meetings allow you to heap peer praise on your top producers. Your top salespeople may not feel they need or appreciate praise and recognition, but they do.

 Monthly sales rallies are the best way to focus your team on your monthly goals and obtain a group commitment to succeed.

Sales managers who conduct five-minute shift rallies everyday notice instant results. Think of yourself as the quarterback. Create a "huddle" before each selling shift. Say, "Okay team, here's what we are going to do today..."

Personal Visits

 The best fertilizer in the garden of business is the boss's footprints.

Too many sales managers develop "ivory tower syndrome." They become so attached to their office projects that they forget what's most important. Nothing is more important than your salesperson's behavior while he or she is with your customers.

When you visit your store, you *see* reality rather than *hear* excuses. No one can tell you that it's slow, or that people aren't buying. You know better.

Your store visits should be both expected and unexpected. When you announce your visits, you provide your salespeople with the opportunity for you to see them at their best, and praise them for it.

Unexpected store visits allow you to see things as they really are. Unexpected visits cause your salespeople to expect the unexpected.

Harry Newhart managed Waikiki's highly successful International Marketplace for over 30 years. Being an ex-Marine officer, he understood discipline and responsibility.

Harry was responsible for the behavior of hundreds of retail entrepreneurs from all over the world. Most of his merchants didn't speak English, and many were unaccustomed to following rules. Harry spoke only English and everyone followed his rules.

Harry's rules were few and simple:
- Open your store on time.
- Wear aloha attire.
- Keep your store clean.
- Be nice to your customers.

The key to Harry's success was his morning walk through the Marketplace. He didn't talk, he just walked and looked. He walked by every store, every day at opening time. He inspected his expectancies. Harry's loyal secretary, Leolani, followed him with a clipboard in her hand.

When Harry walked by someone who was opening late, not wearing aloha attire, or who had a dirty store or a bad attitude, he noticed it. Every system needs a master. Harry was the master of his system.

Harry spotted any dirt, dust, cobwebs, burned-out light bulbs, or broken glass. He would simply point at the problem, Leolani would make a note, and they would continue walking. No excuses!

Following Harry's morning inspection, Leolani sent letters and made phone calls to offending merchants. Sometimes she scheduled an appointment with Harry and the guilty merchant.

Appointments with Harry were unforgettable. No one had very many. I had one. It's still very clear in my mind.

Harry walked by one of my stores and observed an employee not wearing the required aloha shirt. Leolani called the store and told my employee, "Close your store. Lock it up, and wait there for further instructions."

Leolani then called me and said, "Mr. Newhart needs to see you in his office immediately. He has closed one of your stores and needs to discuss it with you in person."

I hurried to Harry's office. He saw me right away. He leaned forward in his chair, furrowed his bushy eyebrows, looked directly at me and asked, "Ron, do you understand our rule that everyone must wear aloha attire while working in the International Marketplace?" I meekly answered, "Yes."

Harry then said, "Well, you apparently failed to communicate the importance of it to one of your employees. I had him close your store. He is waiting for instructions from you."

I said, "Okay, I'll take care of it." Harry smiled and added, "Thank you, and incidentally your lease does not allow your store to be closed. I'll let you go and get it open right now." – End of meeting.

I hustled to my store. My employee was fairly upset. He said he didn't have a clean aloha shirt and thought it would be okay not to wear one, this one time.

I bought him a cheap aloha shirt. I bought five more in different sizes to keep in my office. I also started beating Harry to his morning rounds. I was always ready for him. We became good friends. My stores looked better. I made more money, Harry made more money. My salespeople made more money. Win/win/win.

Harry retired and Leolani assumed his job. Harry's legacy lives on. Salespeople still wear aloha attire in the International Marketplace.

Become the Harry Newhart of your business. Your good people will get better, and your bad ones will leave.

Not everybody loved Harry Newhart. He's been called Harry No Heart. Harry's simple rules had a lot of heart behind them. He cared about his merchants' success, sometimes more so than they did. That's empathy!

Audio and Video Tapes

Audio tapes are inexpensive and easy to create. You can produce a weekly or monthly audio message and distribute it to all of your stores or employees. The tapes can be returned and used again.

Video tapes are an improvement over audio tapes, except that you can't listen to them in your car. Video tapes let you show new merchandise to your salespeople.
You can show your merchandise being manufactured or processed. You can show your new stores to everyone. You can introduce and show new employees to everyone. It's fun.

A monthly or quarterly video magazine is easy to produce. Make it dynamic. Use an editing machine to keep it short.

For your purpose, video content is more important than video quality. You can role-play, capture actual sales on video, and conduct interviews with company executives or top salespeople.

Video magazines should be no more than 30 minutes long. Mix in some music and have fun with it. **It's easy.**

Telephone

The telephone is the least desirable means of salesperson communication. The problem is, you cannot see what's happening on the other end of the line. Customers are sometimes ignored by a salesperson talking on the telephone. Again, when calling your store always ask, "Are you with a customer?", and get off the phone when the answer is "Yes."

A good use of the telephone, or better yet, a beeper, voice mail, e-mail or a fax machine, is to have sales totals called in at designated times throughout the day. This practice keeps everyone focused on selling all day, and lets you know how everyone is doing.

Chapter 11

Managing With "The Boss"

Boss: " ... Exercising control or supervision."
– WEBSTER

"The Boss" is a visual chart that serves as a motivational tool to help you meet your goals. "The Boss" is easy to use. It's as easy as making a dot and drawing a line.

You can use "The Boss" to chart anything you want to improve or accomplish. You can measure your daily, weekly, monthly and annual progress on "The Boss."

 Use "The Boss," to achieve all of your goals.

"The Boss" allows you to *control* sales and *handle* duties. In addition, "The Boss" will motivate your salespeople to achieve their sales goals.

"The Boss" incorporates the major management principle: **If you can measure it, you can manage it**. "The Boss" measures success and allows you to manage it.

"The Boss" puts your priorities in order and keeps you focused on success.

"The Boss" is printed on two-sided card stock. A sample of **"The Boss"** is printed on pages 85 and 86 (figures 1 and 2). **"The Boss"** is also printed at the end of this book to make it easy for you to use. I grant you permission to copy **"The Boss."**

"The Boss" is a visual, silent and effective management tool.

> *"We shape our tools and then our tools shape us."*
> — THOREAU

Side A (figure 1) is your visual road map to your goal. Side B (figure 2) is a record of your daily and accumulated sales, hours worked and sales per hour.

Let's say you own or manage a retail store. You need $80,000 a month in sales, and you have eight salespeople. When each of your eight salespeople achieves $10,000 or more in sales, you reach your goal. **It's easy.**

As the sales manager, you can *hope* every salesperson sells $10,000. Or, you can use **"The Boss"** to make *sure* every salesperson sells $10,000.

 "The Boss" makes your goal everyone's dominant thought.

"**The Boss**" makes $80,000 in sales a reality by keeping each of your salespeople focused and on track all month.

"**The Boss**" overcomes excuses and obstacles along the way. "**The Boss**" silently and consistently demands success. "**The Boss**" makes success easy.

Let's say that your store is open seven days a week and 12 hours a day. That's 372 hours during a 31-day month. You must average $215 per hour in sales to obtain $80,000.

Each salesperson works 184 hours during the month for a total of 1,472 selling hours. To exceed $80,000 in monthly sales, your salespeople must average $55 in sales for each hour worked. That's $440 in sales for an eight-hour shift.

Use "**The Boss**" to track each salesperson's daily sales (figure 3). Draw the goal line (the track) horizontally at $440 then have all of your salespeople plot their actual sales by making a dot and drawing a line everyday (the trail). Instill this discipline in each of your salespeople, and "**The Boss**" will guide them to success. **It's easy.**

Use side B of "**The Boss**" to record and calculate accumulated sales and sales per hour (figure 4).

Your goal is the track.
Your sales are the trail.

Visually display your accumulated sales on side A of "**The Boss**" (figure 5). Notice that this salesperson's accumulated sales line (the trail) remained ahead of the goal line (the track) all month. Total sales for this salesperson were $12,800, well ahead of the $10,000 goal.

You can also use **"The Boss"** to track sales per hour (figure 6). In this example, the goal line (the track) is drawn horizontally at $55 per hour. Daily sales per hour are plotted on the sales line (the trail), and accumulated sales per hour are shaded. **It's easy.**

You can tailor **"The Boss"** to work in conjunction with your company incentive programs and contests. Visually display any goal you establish on side A of **"The Boss."**

 By keeping "The Boss" up-to-date, you convince your subconscious mind that you want to achieve your goal.

Use **"The Boss"** to track your progress towards your store goal (figure 7). To reach $80,000 in sales in 31 days you must average $2,580 a day in sales. Draw your track horizontally at $2,580. Record your daily sales on the trail. In this example you had 10 days of sales under your goal and 21 days over it.

You can also track your accumulated monthly sales for your store (figures 8 and 9). In this example, your total store sales are $94,665. Your goal is $80,000.

Control Sales – Handle Duties.

"The Boss" handles duties. You simply schedule them and **"The Boss"** oversees their timely completion.

For example: You need $80,000 in sales, and you must also:

- Make a bank deposit every Monday, Wednesday and Friday.
- Present an hour-long sales rally every Monday morning.
- Vacuum your store every day.
- Dust your show cases, and mop your show room floors two days a week.
- Clean your store windows once every week.
- Do a visual merchandise inventory 3 days a week.
- Supervise a detailed merchandise inventory every Tuesday.
- Submit a written merchandise inventory once every month.
- Conduct a sales training class every Friday.
- Distribute paychecks twice every month.
- Have a paycheck meeting with each salesperson twice every month.

Some sales managers are intimidated and overwhelmed by the long list of duties they must perform. They object: "... and you expect me to sell too?"

When you use **"The Boss,"** handling duties is as easy as making a dot and drawing a line. You can spread the duties out, and schedule them with a simple dot (figure 10). The dots are crossed out as the duties are completed.

"The Boss" (figure 10) shows that today is Friday the 12th and you've got a busy day. But, you can go to the bank in the morning, assign cleaning duties, prepare for your training class, then sell and coach for most of the day. **It's easy.**

Instead of dots, you can use your employees' initials to assign duties. The duties will be handled, but not at the expense of sales.

With **"The Boss"** on the job, everyone will exceed $10,000 in sales, your store will exceed $80,000 in sales, and all duties will be done as well. **It's easy.**

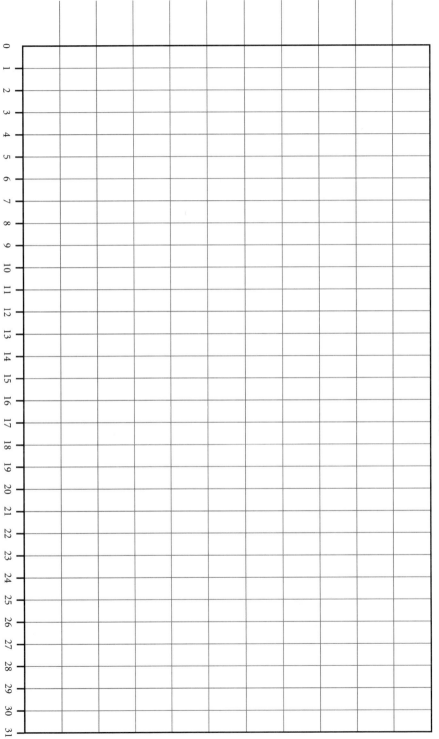

"THE BOSS"

Figure 1

DAILY SALES LOG

NAME: _____ MONTH _____ GOAL _____

DAILY SALES		CUMULATIVE SALES	
1.	_____	1.	_____
2.	_____	2.	_____
3.	_____	3.	_____
4.	_____	4.	_____
5.	_____	5.	_____
6.	_____	6.	_____
7.	_____	7.	_____
8.	_____	8.	_____
9.	_____	9.	_____
10.	_____	10.	_____
11.	_____	11.	_____
12.	_____	12.	_____
13.	_____	13.	_____
14.	_____	14.	_____
15.	_____	15.	_____
16.	_____	16.	_____
17.	_____	17.	_____
18.	_____	18.	_____
19.	_____	19.	_____
20.	_____	20.	_____
21.	_____	21.	_____
22.	_____	22.	_____
23.	_____	23.	_____
24.	_____	24.	_____
25.	_____	25.	_____
26.	_____	26.	_____
27.	_____	27.	_____
28.	_____	28.	_____
29.	_____	29.	_____
30.	_____	30.	_____
31.	_____	31.	_____

Figure 2

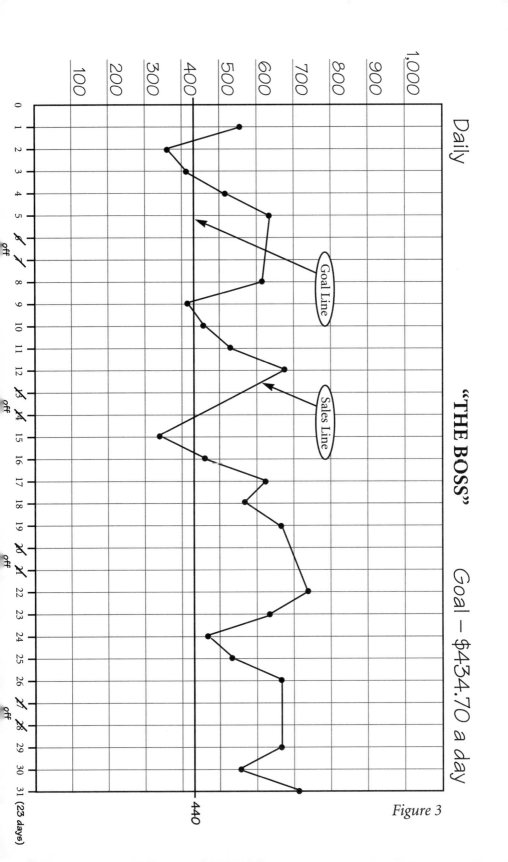

Daily   "THE BOSS"   Goal – $434.70 a day

Figure 3

DAILY SALES LOG

NAME _____ MONTH _____ GOAL <u>55.00 per hour</u>

	DAILY SALES				**CUMULATIVE SALES**		
	HRS	SALES	PER HR		HRS	SALES	PER HR
1.	8	550	68.70	1.	8	550	68.70
2.	8	380	47.50	2.	16	930	58.10
3.	8	410	51.20	3.	24	1340	55.80
4.	8	520	65.00	4.	32	1860	58.10
5.	8	640	80.00	5.	40	2500	62.50
6.				6.			
7.				7.			
8.	8	610	76.20	8.	48	3110	64.70
9.	8	420	52.50	9.	56	3530	63.00
10.	8	450	56.20	10.	64	3980	62.10
11.	8	530	66.20	11.	72	4510	62.60
12.	8	680	85.00	12.	80	5190	64.80
13.				13.			
14.				14.			
15.	8	340	42.50	15.	88	5530	62.80
16.	8	480	60.00	16.	96	6010	62.60
17.	8	610	76.20	17.	104	6620	63.60
18.	8	580	72.50	18.	112	7200	64.20
19.	8	650	81.20	19.	120	7850	65.40
20.				20.			
21.				21.			
22.	8	740	92.50	22.	128	8590	67.10
23.	8	610	76.20	23.	136	9200	67.60
24.	8	480	60.00	24.	144	9680	67.20
25.	8	510	63.70	25.	152	10,190	67.00
26.	8	680	85.00	26.	160	10,870	67.90
27.				27.			
28.				28.			
29.	8	680	85.00	29.	168	11,550	68.70
30.	8	540	67.50	30.	176	12,090	68.60
31.	8	710	88.70	31.	184	12,800	69.50

Sales Management Made Easy © Success Dynamics, Inc. • Honolulu, Hawaii 1966

Figure 4

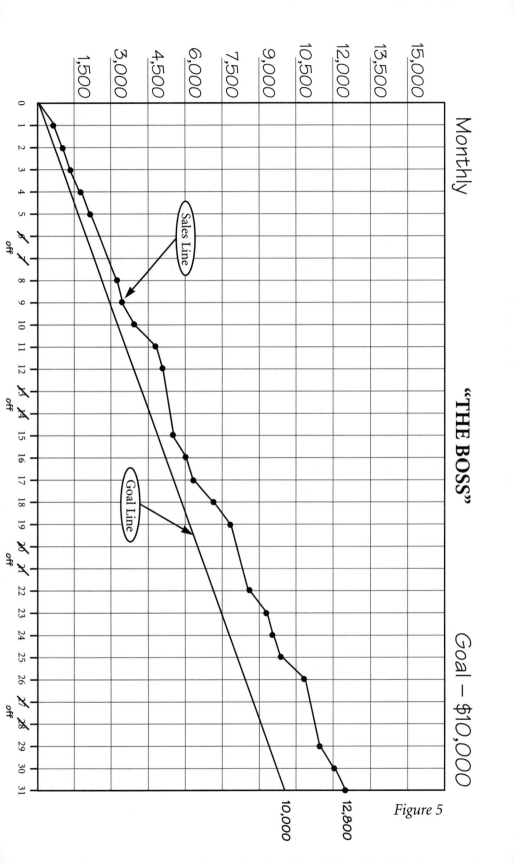

Monthly   "THE BOSS"   Goal – $10,000

Figure 5

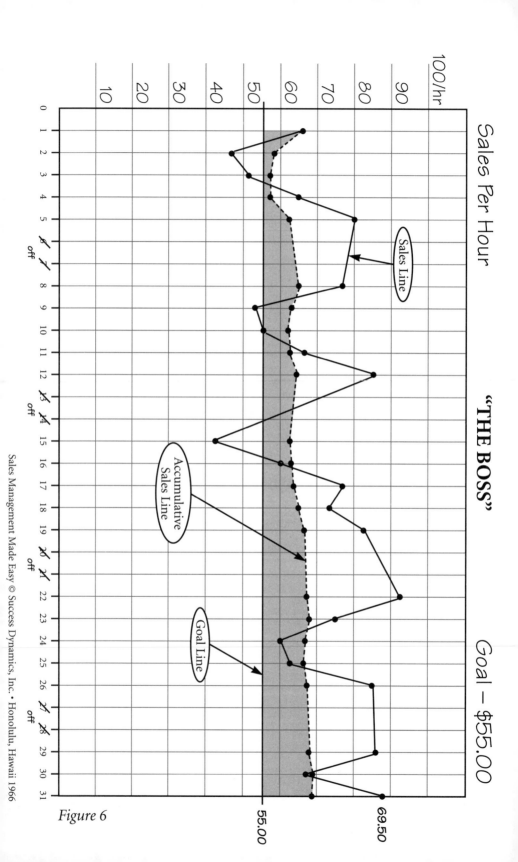

Sales Per Hour   "THE BOSS"   Goal – $55.00

Sales Line

Accumulative Sales Line

Goal Line

55.00

69.50

Figure 6

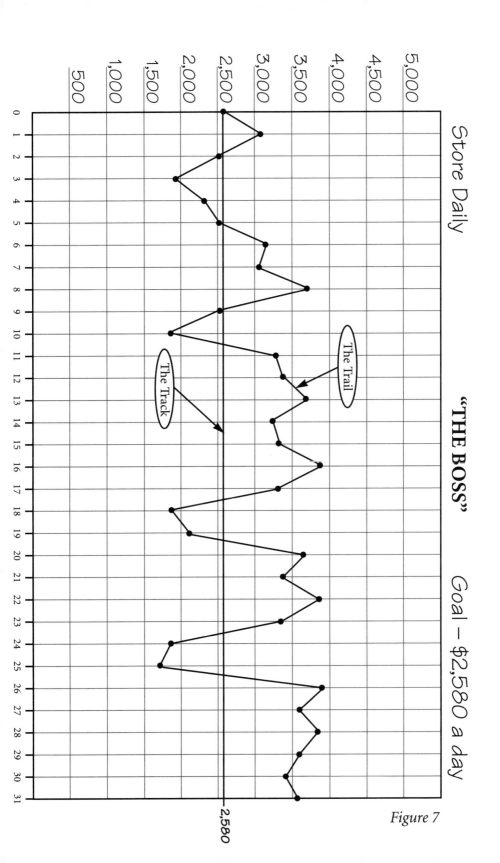

Figure 7

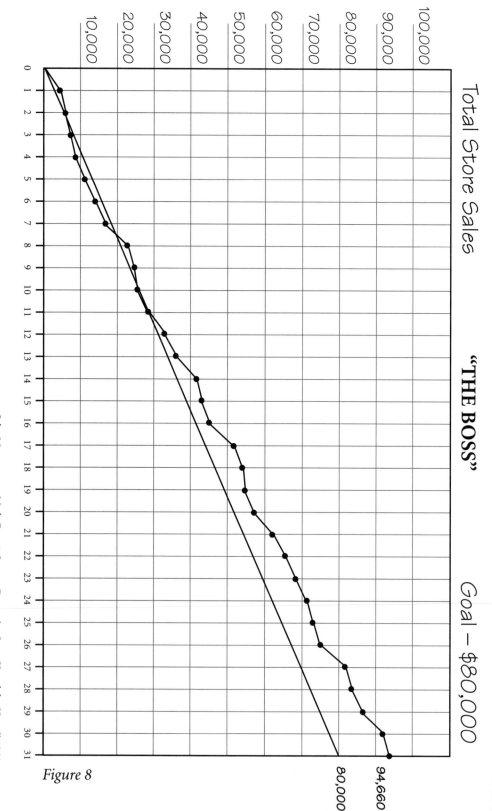

Total Store Sales   "THE BOSS"   Goal – $80,000

100,000
90,000
80,000
70,000
60,000
50,000
40,000
30,000
20,000
10,000

0 1 2 3 4 5 6 7 8 9 10 11 12 13 14 15 16 17 18 19 20 21 22 23 24 25 26 27 28 29 30 31

94,660
80,000

Figure 8

Sales Management Made Easy © Success Dynamics, Inc. • Honolulu, Hawaii 1966

DAILY SALES LOG

NAME _Store_   MONTH _March_   GOAL _80,000_

	DAILY SALES		CUMULATIVE SALES
1.	3,026.50	1.	3,026.50
2.	2,413.20	2.	5,439.70
3.	1,908.10	3.	7,347.80
4.	2,348.90	4.	9,696.70
5.	2,412.90	5.	12,109.60
6.	3,240.10	6.	15,349.70
7.	3,120.40	7.	18,470.10
8.	3,714.10	8.	22,184.20
9.	2,550.10	9.	24,734.30
10.	1,815.90	10.	26,550.10
11.	3,320.50	11.	29,870.60
12.	3,410.50	12.	33,281.11
13.	3,750.10	13.	37,031.20
14.	3,250.20	14.	40,281.40
15.	3,425.10	15.	43,706.50
16.	3,890.50	16.	47,597.00
17.	3,310.80	17.	50,907.80
18.	1,910.20	18.	52,818.00
19.	2,010.10	19.	54,828.10
20.	3,620.50	20.	58,448.60
21.	3,450.10	21.	61,898.70
22.	3,850.20	22.	65,748.90
23.	3,350.10	23.	69,099.00
24.	1,850.40	24.	70,949.40
25.	1,740.10	25.	72,689.50
26.	3,950.20	26.	76,639.70
27.	3,520.50	27.	80,160.20
28.	3,842.10	28.	84,002.30
29.	3,612.50	29.	87,614.80
30.	3,450.20	30.	91,065.00
31.	3,600.00	31.	94,665.00

Sales Management Made Easy © Success Dynamics, Inc. • Honolulu, Hawaii 1966

Figure 9

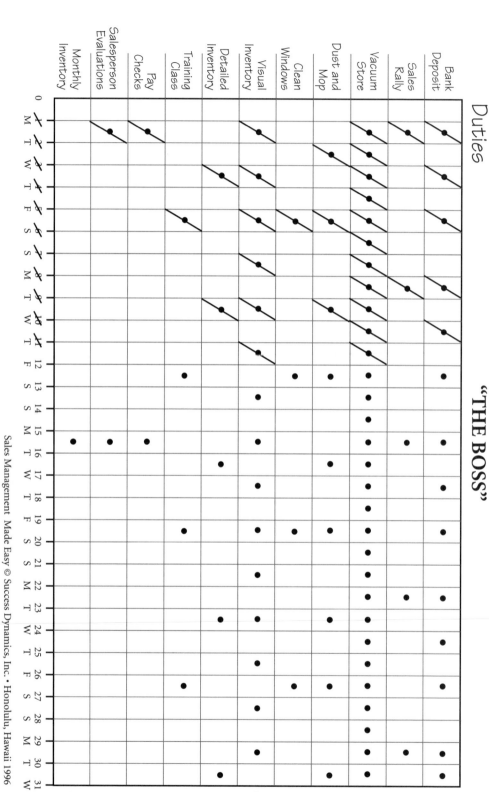

Duties   "THE BOSS"

Sales Management Made Easy © Success Dynamics, Inc. • Honolulu, Hawaii 1996

Figure 10

Chapter 12

Managing Failure

"Failure is a highly contagious disease."
– Paul Newman, in "Sweet Bird of Youth"

When you teach, motivate, encourage, coach, council, mentor and even pressure people to succeed, and they don't, *you* have a problem.

Bad apples will spoil the entire barrel. Allowing an underachiever to remain on your team delivers the wrong message to everyone else.

The toughest job in management is firing someone, but someone's got to do it. It feels awful at the time, but successful managers know that sometimes it's in everyone's best interest.

"Failures are like skinned knees – painful but superficial."
– Ross Perot

Even more difficult than firing someone is deciding *if* and *when* to. It's a dilemma. You don't want to fire a salesperson who is on the verge of success. On the other hand, you don't want to keep a salesperson who will never succeed.

When you allow people to fail in your business, you are preventing them from succeeding elsewhere. And, you are denying yourself the opportunity to hire someone who will succeed in your business, and help your business grow.

 It's a lose/lose situation when you keep a loser.

When deciding whether or not to fire someone, take a personal inventory first. Have you done *your* job? Have you done everything within your power to help this person succeed? Have you communicated your displeasure along the way? Will this firing be expected? If so, it's probably necessary. If so, it will be a win/win. You can hire a winner, and your departing salesperson can find a job where he or she will win.

When you are *certain* that it's time for a change say, "Everyone deserves to be successful at something. You are not succeeding here. I must make a change. Here is your final paycheck."

Many sales managers are so uncomfortable with firing someone that they allow failures to hang around, and then abuse them hoping they will quit. Lose/lose.

"Delays have dangerous ends."

— SHAKESPEARE

 Don't punish failures; release them to succeed elsewhere.

Most people who are failing are not sufficiently motivated to quit and seek another job. They hang on, and do their best to keep their jobs. They need your help. You must have empathy, not sympathy for people who fail. Help them succeed, or help them move on.

When you are not sure which direction to take, serve up a "hot bowl of soup," and find out. If the cook in a restaurant served you a bowl of soup that was too hot to eat, what would you do? Would you scream at the cook, or would you let it cool off a bit?

 You don't have to eat the soup as hot as you serve it.

Say something stronger than you mean to. Touch a nerve. Find out what this salesperson is made of. Say: "Suzie, I've been analyzing your performance, and I'm afraid I *might* be holding you back. Everyone can succeed somewhere, and you are not succeeding here. I was thinking that *maybe* we both *might be* better off *if* I made a change. What do *you* think?"

Emphasize the italicized words, and then be quiet. You'll find out what's truly inside of your salesperson. **It's easy.**

Salespeople who *expect* to be fired, and are just hanging on to their paychecks, won't hear your emphasized words. Rather than hear: "maybe," "might" and "if," they only hear: "performance," "not succeeding" and "change." They think: "It's all over."

Failures cave in. They make your job easy. They say: "Yeah, you're right. I was looking for a job when I found this one." Or, they explode. They protest: "Hey, I'm not the only one that's not selling. It's not my fault. It's slow. It's the economy. People aren't buying."

Either response lets you know that you are on the right course – change. Do it now! Prepare this person's final check. Keep it positive and friendly. Say, "Feel free to use me as a reference. I know you'll succeed when you find the right job. Good luck."

On the other hand salespeople who want to keep their jobs and believe that success is just around the corner will hear your emphasized words, "maybe," "might" and "if" loud and clear. They plead: "Don't give up on me. I know I can do it. I just need a little more time and a little more help. Please give me another chance."

When you get a response like this, you may have a winner on your hands after all. You may have someone worth keeping. You may have a winner who needed a wake-up call. Some people slip all the way down to the end of the rope before climbing back up.

 A job worth begging for is a job worth working for.

When someone begs to keep his or her job, say: "Don't get me wrong. I'd much rather help *you* succeed than have to train a new salesperson. However, there are some areas you are going to have to improve in. If I work with you, are you willing to work on these areas?"

When the answer is "yes," launch a renewed learning and coaching effort. However, keep in mind that the habits that have led to failure so far may be stronger than the intentions to change.

It's a good practice to document these discussions in your salesperson's employee file. Never establish a set probation time. Say, "Okay, we'll watch it day-by-day and see how you do."

"Yanagi Ni Kaze," is a Japanese proverb that says: "Wind in the willow tree." The slim willow tree bends while the wind blows, but goes right back where it was when the wind stops blowing. Think about it.

Chapter 13

Managing Success

"Success or failure lies in conforming to the times."

— MACHIAVELLI

To succeed, you need a selling system that ensures sales success, and a management system that stimulates ongoing and ever-increasing success.

Be sure your sales and management systems make sales your #1 priority. Develop systems that:

- Teach selling.
- Encourage leadership.
- Motivate salesperson growth.
- Prioritize salesperson activities.
- Overcome obstacles.
- Incorporate salesperson incentives.
- Offer contests.
- Regulate training.
- Institutionalize communication.
- Feed the winners.
- Starve the losers.
- Use **"The Boss"**.

If you need a system that delivers all of the above, consider using the Success Dynamics Sales Training System. It works. **It's easy.**

Success Dynamics Sales Training System

First impressions are lasting impressions. This is true with your customers and also with your new salespeople.

Ask retailers what they teach a new salesperson first, and most will answer, "How to use the cash register." A major department store in Honolulu starts every new salesperson with two full days of cash register training. In doing so, this store "tells" its salespeople that clerking is their most important task and they become good clerks. When their customers find what they want and walk to a register, the clerk does a good job of ringing it up.

Shoppers at this store who need help won't get it unless they ask for it. The salespeople are functional clerks, they have not been taught how to sell.

Many managers teach the cash register first so they can leave their new salespeople alone. They believe their salespeople are trained fully because they are able to ring up sales.

Cash register training can be stressful. The cash register is complicated and frustrating. Some companies invest several hours training new salespeople how to use the cash register, only to see them quit when they have to sell.

A salesperson who can't sell doesn't need cash register training.

The Success Dynamics Training System consists of 12 easy steps which make selling most important by teaching selling first and by treating salespeople like career professionals.

Step 1

On the first day, each new salesperson reads Retail Selling Made Easy, by yours truly, cover to cover. This takes two to three hours. It's easy to read. It says, "Selling comes first." Meanwhile the manager returns to selling and managing.

Step 2

The new salesperson takes an open book quiz. The quiz consists of three or more questions on each book chapter. The store manager writes the quiz questions.

The quiz is your opportunity to tailor the book information to your store. The quiz makes your new salesperson think about the most important points of each chapter, look them up, reread them, and write them down. This assures learning.

The first two steps of this system usually occupy three to four hours of the first day. Your new salesperson is learning how to sell while you are doing other work.

Your new salespeople don't have to strain their brains on the register, yet. Anyone with a good attitude can read a book and pass an open book quiz.

"Retail Selling Made Easy" teaches the easy-to-follow, nine-step system: Pro-Active, No-Pressure Selling. Part of this system is a very important tool, "The Sale City Express" (figure 11).

Step 3

The sales manager questions the new salesperson's understanding of how to use "The Sale City Express." "The Sale City Express" is a simple checklist of the steps that are taken to make each sale.

The sales manager makes sure the new salesperson understands how to use this tool by reviewing the completed example of "The Sale City Express" on page 126 of Retail Selling Made Easy (figure 12). The sales manager asks, "What do you think happened with customer #1, #2, #3,?" etc. The sales manager reviews all 10 customer examples with the new salesperson.

Step 4

The new salesperson goes to the store and records observations of actual sales being made on "The Sale City Express".

The sales manager advises, "Be a 'mouse in the corner.' When a customer enters the store, just watch. If the salesperson greets the customer in the manner you read about on page 32, then check the #1 box on 'The Sale City Express.' Keep watching and check off the steps as they are taken. Observe 10 customers from beginning to end. Total 'The Sale City Express,' and call me." The sales manager returns to selling and managing.

Depending upon how busy your store is, this step may conclude the first day. Your new salesperson has not experienced any stress, has learned a lot about selling and used very little of your time.

Step 5

The sales manager reviews each of the 10 customer experiences observed by the new salesperson. The manager asks, "What happened with customer #1, #2, #3,?" etc. New salespeople say things like: "She did it just like in the book." Or, "He wasn't following the system."

New salespeople recognize right from wrong. They learn the right way regardless of the examples they observe.

Without this process, your new salespeople might see wrong behavior and think it's right. They might observe shortcuts being taken and think they are improvements to your system.

Step 6

The sales manager tells the new salesperson: "Okay, it's your turn. It's time for you to face 10 customers of your own. Just follow the system you've been learning. I'll be there with you. I'll observe, and record the steps you take on the ' The Sale City Express.' If you get in trouble, I'll help you. If you make a sale, I'll ring it up for you. I mainly want you to get comfortable talking with customers."

Step 7

The sales manager reviews his or her observations of the 10 customers with the new salesperson. New salespeople enjoy this process. It's rewarding and reassuring for them to review their early performance and discuss their feelings and fears with managers who care.

This step ends with a review of the totals across the bottom of "The Sale City Express." The sales manager says, "Your goal is to consistently increase your average total sales with 10 customers. You do it by increasing the total number of people you greet, by giving more information, and by improving your ability to follow each step in the system."

Step 8

The new salesperson is now ready to "fly solo." The sales manager says, "Okay, you're on your own. Handle 10 customers from beginning to end. Complete the 'The Sale City Express' and then call me."

Step 9

The sales manager reviews " The Sale City Express" with the new salesperson. The sales manager asks, "What happened with customers #1, #2, #3,?" etc. They discuss each customer experience, step-by-step, and compare the totals to the first "Sale City Express."

Step 10

The sales manager gives the new salesperson a copy of the book Success Made Easy, by yours truly, and says, "Read this book cover to cover, and call me when you finish. I'll have another quiz for you."

Step 11

The new salesperson takes an open book quiz on Success Made Easy. Again, the sales manager prepares the quiz, tailoring the questions to his or her store.

Step 12

The sales manager coaches the new salesperson through the goal setting process. **"The Boss"** is re-introduced and explained. Goals are established and displayed on **"The Boss."**

Future steps in this process include:
- Daily reviews of **"The Boss"**.
- Weekly analysis of "The Sale City Express".
- Monthly goal setting sessions.

Success Made Easy, Retail Selling Made Easy, and **Sales Management Made Easy** comprise a trilogy for your selling success. It's a system. It works, and **it's easy.**

THE SALE CITY EXPRESS

	Greet	Position	Speak	Tell	Show	Overcome	Nudge	Add-On	Befriend	$ Total
	1	**2**	**3**	**4**	**5**	**6**	**7**	**8**	**9**	**$**
1										
2										
3										
4										
5										
6										
7										
8										
9										
10										
Totals										**$**

CUSTOMERS

Sales Management Made Easy © Success Dynamics, Inc. • Honolulu, Hawaii 1966

Figure 11

THE SALE CITY EXPRESS

– Example –

	Greet	Position	Speak	Tell	Show	Overcome	Nudge	Add-On	Befriend	$ Total
	1	**2**	**3**	**4**	**5**	**6**	**7**	**8**	**9**	**$**
1	✓	✓	✓	✓	✓	✓	✓	✓	✓	$100
2	✓	✓	✓	✓	✓			✓	✓	$80
3					✓			✓	✓	$50
4	✓	✓	✓					✓	✓	$70
5									✓	$10
6	✓		✓	✓	✓	✓	✓		✓	θ
7	✓	✓	✓	✓	✓	✓			✓	$80
8	✓	✓	✓	✓						θ
9						✓	✓	✓	✓	✓	$40
10	✓	✓	✓	✓	✓	✓			✓	$90
Totals	7	6	7	6	7	5	3	5	9	**$520**

CUSTOMERS

Retail Selling Made Easy © Success Dynamics, Inc. • Honolulu, Hawaii 1966

Figure 12

Success Dynamics
Sales Training System
12-Step Checklist

❑ 1. Read Retail Selling Made Easy by Ron Martin.

❑ 2. Take an open book quiz on Retail Selling Made Easy.

❑ 3. Understand how to use the "The Sale City Express."

❑ 4. Observe 10 customers, and record your observations on "The Sale City Express."

❑ 5. Review your 10-customer observations with your sales manager.

❑ 6. Face 10 customers of your own with your sales manager observing and recording your progress on "The Sale City Express."

❑ 7. Review your observations of these 10 customers with those of your sales manager.

❑ 8. "Fly solo" with 10 customers and record your behavior on "The Sale City Express."

❑ 9. Review the results of your "solo flight" with your sales manager.

❑ 10. Read Success Made Easy by Ron Martin.

❑ 11. Take an open book quiz on Success Made Easy.

❑ 12. Set your goals using **"The Boss."**

Use this Success Dynamics Training System as is, or modify it to supplement some other successful training and selling system that works for you. In any case, plan your success. Success is no accident.

- Enjoy Success
- Sell – Sell – Sell
- Make A Difference. **It's easy.**

The End

Acknowledgements

I am deeply indebted to the many people who have made this book possible.

Mahalo to:

Tom O'Gwynn – For showing me how to eliminate needless paperwork and increase sales.

Hal Johnson – For showing me the importance of structured management.

Ruby Pollock – For her never-ending patience as I revised my changes over and over, again and again.

Doug Behrens – For turning my ideas into reality on both the inside and the outside of another book.

Kenny Williams – For capturing another "moment" on another cover.

Dick Lyday – For transforming another manuscript into more boxes of books.

And to:

Rich Budnick – Becky Ehling – Betty Ling – Guillaume Mamon – Ed Randolph – Ed Schneider – Brick Thompson
for their editorial advice and assistance.

Mahalo also to the business owners and sales managers who have allowed me to demonstrate how to make sales the most important function they manage.

Jan Amos	Eddie Crawford
Richard Amos	Ed D'Ascoli
Simone Andrade	Karen D'Ascoli
Fritz Arko	Heidi Di Eugenio
Sandie Arntzen	Clara Dias
Bill Barnfield	Don Dixon
Wendy Barnfield	Mark Doo
Lynn Becker	Corinne Dumas
Jan Berman	Dave Dumas
Maggie Breeden	Mark Ellman
Paul Brown	Jip Englis
Diane Bruce	Marc Eremian
Claudia Cannon	Becky Erickson
Michael Castillo	Pam Farley
Jeff Castle	Gloria Fazendin
Judy Castle	Beverly Fettig
Pam Chambers	Kulani Fernandez
Kathy Chan	Linda Fernandez
Bob Chilton	Julia Ferreira
Dee Chapman	Michael Fieman
Annette Clay	Audrey Foo
Darcy Cook	Mary Flood
Howard Cook	Ann Franzman
Ron Courtney	Harry Fujita

Vince Gannon

Jim Geiger

Jo Grande

Guy Grande

Joe Green

Deborah Greene

Bob Gunter

Sutji Gunter

Lee Hacohen

David Hagerman

Clyde Hamai

Scott Head

Wayne Hedani

Fred Hendeles

Lazare Hendeles

Diana Hillier

Debbie Hind

Steve Hofer

Clyde Horikami

Bill Indich

Armond Jackson

Richard Jacobs

Hal Johnson

Carl Johnson

Lloyd Jones

Alexandra Kaaua

Marty Kahn

Carol Kahn

Leslee Kanaiaupuni

Lynn Kaninau

Kathy Kameda

Oscar Kawahara

Charles Kawakami

Don Kelly

Mary Kelly

Uncle Billy Kimi

Billy Kimi

Jeannie Kimi

Kimo Kimi

Laura Kimi

Kenneth Kimura

Leolani Kini

Mel Kitagawa

Cheryl Kojima

Cheryl Konrad

Howard Konrad

Minnie Kosasa

Paul Kosasa

Sydney Kosasa

Robert Kotcher

Jeff Kramer

Sam Kramer

Masago Kumagai

Valerie Lamoureux

Gail Lee

Larry Lee

Linda Lee

Gwen LeBlanc

Tom Leppert

Jim Lightner

Bob Linau

Kimberly Lord

Jill Mackie

Michael Martin

Higgins Maddigan

Guillaume Mamon

Susan Martinson

Max Massanari

Melvin Matsuoka

Ricky McCann

Laurie McCarty

Claudia McCotter

John McCotter

Jim McGuinness

Michelle McGuinness

Stuart Mckenzie

Frank Mento

Gordon Miller

Norman Miller

Tao Miller

Dave Mitchell

Colin Miyabara

Ela Moniuszko

Mahmoud Monpoir

Mike Moon

Bob Moore

Angela Morehead

Joel Murphy

Tiffany Murphy

Sharon Naeole

Willie Nishii

Steve Norstrom

Valery O'Brien

Troy Ochiai

Sandi Oguma

Tom O'Gwynn

Lori Okamura

Don Olson

Lorna Ouderkirk

Cleigh Pang

Art Parent

Patricia Parent

Paki Perkins

Ramona Perkins

Robin Peterson

Charlie Pietsch III

Jeff Pietsch

Valerie Pichler

Steve Pogni	Jack Stevenson
Aness Pogni	Ed Sultan Jr.
Bill Powell	Ed Sultan III
Telle Presley	Jeff Swartz
John Pyles	Cindy Tagavilla
Kelly Reed	Guy Takahashi
Don Reeser	Margo Takata
Howard Richie	Jean Tantano
Ron Robertson	Robert Taylor
Billy Robillard	Brick Thompson
Rhonda Roldan	Tamara Timoshik
Jean Rolles	Suzanne Todd
Roy Sakai	Masae Trevino
Shenai Sakai	Jill Tsu
Paul Sato	Stephen Tsukayama
Ed Schneider	Jimmy Tsukayama
John Schuyler	Jennifer Uradomo
Kathleen Scott	Kent Untermann
Tom Shaw	Lori Untermann
Yana Shayne	Kimberly Van Arsdale
Crawford Sherman	Doug Victorino
Mario Simic	Bernard von NotHaus
Cliff Slater	Lahela Waiwaiole
Doug Smoyer	Alan Walker
Elizabeth Snavely	Charline Walker
Terry Snavely	Merrill Walker
Donna Soares	Bernard Walthall

Ed Wayne

Bill Welsh

Helga Wheeler

Tina White

Gilbert Wizeman

Kelly Wong

Lucien Wong

Richard Wong

Akiko Woolliams

Charlian Wright

Wyland

Bill Wyland

Darlene Wyland

Sandy Yokomizo

Patti Zada

Ray Zada

Ordering Information

You may obtain additional copies of Sales Management
Made Easy from your favorite bookstore or:

Success Dynamics, Inc.
P.O. Box 489
Haleiwa, HI 96712

Phone: (808) 637-5020
Fax: (808) 637-4914
e-mail: easy@aloha.net

Write, call, fax or e-mail us to request more information
about these books:

Success Made Easy by Ron Martin

Retail Selling Made Easy by Ron Martin

Sales Management Made Easy by Ron Martin

Public Speaking Made Easy by Pam Chambers
                              – with Ron Martin